My Fat Cat

Ten Simple Steps to Help Your Pet
Lose Weight for a Long and Happy Life

D1445731

My Fat Cat

Ten Simple Steps to Help Your Pet Lose Weight for a Long and Happy Life

Martha Garvey

Foreword by Deborah Greco, D.V.M., Ph.D.,
The Animal Medical Center

Illustrations by Sebastian Conley

healthyliving**books**

New York • London

A Healthy Living Book
Published by Hatherleigh Press
5-22 46th Avenue, Suite 200
Long Island City, NY 11101
www.hatherleighpress.com

Library of Congress Cataloging-in-Publication Data

Garvey, Martha.
  My fat cat : ten simple steps to help your pet lose weight for a long and happy life / Martha Garvey ; foreword by Deborah Greco.
     p. cm.
  Includes bibliographical references.
  ISBN 1-57826-197-X
  1. Cats--Diseases--Diet therapy. 2. Cats--Exercise. 3. Cats--Health. 4. Obesity in animals. I. Title.
  SF985.G33 2005
  636.8'0895854--dc22

                          2005012408

Disclaimer
The information in this book is meant to be used under the supervision of a veterinarian, and you should get approval before beginning a regimen. The author, editors, and publisher disclaim any liability or loss in connection with the use of this book or advice within.

All Healthy Living Books are available for bulk purchase, special promotions, and premiums. For information on reselling and special purchase opportunities, call 1-800-528-2550 and ask for the Special Sales Manager.

Interior design by Deborah Miller, Phillip Mondestin, Jacinta Monniere
Cover design by Deborah Miller & Phillip Mondestin

10 9 8 7 6 5 4 3 2 1
Printed in Canada

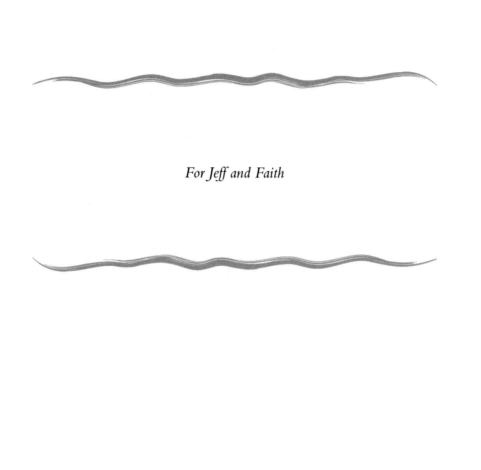

For Jeff and Faith

Contents

Acknowledgments

No book ever gets written without the help of lots of fantastic people (and in this book's case, a few great cats). Thanks to everyone who told me their stories, shared pictures, provided diet and training tips, and just plain loved their cats. Thank you to: Janine Adams, Dr. Phil Brown, Bill Bishop, Susan Chenelle, Joyce Darrell, Renee Deluca, Dr. Aine McCarthy, Janice Livingston, Dr. Andrew Kaplan, Stephen Payne, Raluca State, Sue Gilsdorf, Dr. Bob Goldstein, Jennifer Teitler, Dr. Emily Levine, Koren Wetmore, Dr. Jennifer Jellison, Dr. Martha Gearhart, Mark Robinson, Vickie Shields, Tammy Levitt, the staff at the Liberty Humane Shelter, the Assisi Center, Beowoof, Animal Pantry and the Hoboken Public Library, and finally, my online human companions at Freelance Success, Readerville, and the Utne Café.

Extra special thanks to Stephany Evans, intrepid agent and great dog mom, and Andrea Au, clear-eyed, cat-loving editor.

Foreword

It is estimated that more than 100 million Americans are overweight and that 25 to 45 percent of our pets are overweight. So the question is why? Is it lack of exercise, consumption of fast food, high fat, or high carbohydrate diets?

A recent film documentary, "Super Size Me," chronicles the journey of a healthy 185 pound, 6 ft., 2 in. man who embarks on a fast-food odyssey of epic (or super-sized) proportions. Protagonist Morgan Spurlock consumes all his meals at McDonald's for one month, despite protests from his girlfriend (a vegan), his doctors and yes, even his stomach (he begins vomiting out the window of his car soon after instituting "le diet"). Unfortunately his body and health are on the losing end of this project: He gains weight, his liver becomes toxic, his cholesterol increases, his libido sags, and he becomes depressed. Aptly, he describes the unique combination of hunger and revulsion familiar to those of us who have eaten bite after bite of calorie-laden, nutrient-poor fast food.

Clearly fast food isn't the cause of feline obesity—or is it? What is the equivalent of a kitty Big Mac? Could it be the tower of dry cat food lurking in the corner? It's convenient (like fast food), it's full of carbohydrates (like fast food), and it's available 24 hours a day (like fast food). In the wild, cats maintain normal to low body weight because they do not overfeed. In the wild, mice are the primary component of a feline diet. The body composition of a mouse is approximately 45-50% protein, 3-5% carbohydrate, and 40-45% fat. In other words, cats thrive on a low-carbohydrate, high-protein diet. One of the theories behind feline obesity is that cats overeat in an effort to maintain adequate protein levels in their diet.

Why be concerned about obesity in our cats? Like human beings, obese cats are over four times more likely than optimal weight cats to become diabetic, arthritic, and have non-allergic skin disease. Indoor, neutered, middle-aged cats—like our beloved pets—are especially at risk for obesity.

Indoor cats tend to do very little in the way of physical activity and most owners are at a loss about how to get them to exercise. But there are indeed ways to make your cat move! You may even be able to take your cat for a walk. In addition, you can easily adjust your cat's diet by measuring portions and emphasizing high-protein foods. In *My Fat Cat*, Martha Garvey outlines a simple and effective approach to weight loss in cats and gives practical tips on instituting that approach, even if you have a lazy older cat who is set in his ways or a house full of energetic kittens prone to swiping all the other pets' food. *My Fat Cat* is an excellent and much-needed resource for anyone who needs help taking weight off their corpulent kitty.

—Deborah Greco, D.V.M., Ph.D.

Deborah Greco, D.V.M., Ph.D., is currently a staff endocrinologist at The Animal Medical Center in New York. The recipient of the Pfizer award for research excellence and the American Association of Feline Practitioners research award for her work on feline diabetes mellitus, Dr. Greco was a professor of small animal internal medicine at Colorado State University for twelve years. A diplomate of the American College of Veterinary Internal Medicine, she received her D.V.M. from the University of California and her Ph.D. from Texas A&M University.

Find Out If Your Cat Is Really Fat

Usually, you're the last to know. You raised your cat from a tiny ball of fluff to a lithe adult. Then, a friend comes over and gently comments on your tabby's extra tummy. And you have to admit, as your beloved feline companion ambles from chair to floor and back again—he isn't exactly moving as quickly as he used to. And there's more of him than there used to be. Could your cat be fat?

Nobody gets fat overnight, not even a cat. At an average weight of six to 12 pounds, cats do have less leeway than humans before they become obese. Still, most overweight cats gain the weight the same way humans do. They slowly put on the pounds over the course of a few months, or even years. A few extra treats here, a little less activity there, and eventually, your cat isn't the slender athlete who races from room to room any more. He's a fat cat.

Don't feel bad. You're not alone. In fact, if you live in the United States, you're part of a trend. According to a comprehensive 450-page report on pet obesity published by the National Academies' National Research Council in 2003, "One out of every four dogs and cats in the western world is now obese."

But while the image of the fat, happy cat is ubiquitous (some vets even refer to "the Garfield syndrome"), the long-term impact of fat on your cat is very, very bad.

Excess weight puts pressure on the cat's joints, which means your formerly frisky cat moves less, and may even put himself at risk for injury, particularly if your cat can no longer jump the way he used to.

Excess weight means that your cat may no longer be able to groom himself thoroughly. A cat's self-grooming regimen serves several important functions, including cooling him off in the hot weather, sloughing off dead hair, soothing him, and stimulating the sebaceous glands, which waterproof a cat's fur, and provide the cat with a small amount of vitamin D. When a long-haired cat under-grooms, it can lead to hair mats, which restrict the cat's movement, and may even lead to a fungal or bacterial infection. Overweight cats both short-haired and long-haired frequently miss spots that they used to clean; in extreme cases, these areas may even attract flies. A responsible owner should be grooming his cat on a regular schedule already, but if your cat becomes overweight, it becomes imperative.

Excess weight puts your cat at greater risk for a host of diseases, including diabetes, arthritis, and skin disorders.

WHEN CATS GET FAT: THE CONSEQUENCES

When a cat becomes significantly overweight, he may look perfectly happy and healthy. But a fat cat often is a medical time bomb. Here are some of the problems he may have.

Diabetes. Diabetes is highly treatable, and many diabetic cats lead long and healthy lives. Diabetes occurs in a cat when there is a very high concentration of sugar in the blood and urine. There are two types of diabetes: in insulin-dependent diabetes, the pancreas fails to produce enough insulin to regulate blood sugar levels; in non-insulin-dependent diabetes, the body does not respond to the insulin the pancreas produces. In both situations, the result is that the cat's system literally feeds on the cat's muscle and fat because of its inability to metabolize glucose. Symptoms of diabetes include weight loss, ravenous hunger, increased urination, elimination outside the litter box, and heightened thirst. Diabetes is diagnosed with a blood test, administered by your vet. As with humans, diabetic cats are usually treated with daily insulin injections, although some diabetic cats do respond well to orally-administered drugs, and others do improve with a modified diet.

Arthritis. Arthritis is a broad term for a category of illnesses that strike cats when their joints become inflamed. The most common forms are traumatic arthritis and osteoarthritis. Traumatic arthritis occurs when your cat suffers a sudden injury to a joint, following, for example, a bad fall, a cat fight, or a car accident. Symptoms include a swollen or painful joint. There is no question that your fat cat's extra weight can and does have an impact both on the severity of his injury and on his recovery progress. Treatment usually includes rest, anti-inflammatories, supportive dressings, and, less frequently, surgery.

Symptoms of osteoarthritis include limping, an abnormally-shaped joint, and even lameness. Treatment includes anti-inflammatories, exercise, diet management, and, when necessary, surgery. It's especially important that you, as a cat owner, commit to changing your cat's fitness and food lifestyle if he suffers from osteoarthritis. Don't let your cat sleep for hours. Encourage his movement. Monitor his diet. And remember that a lighter cat is a more physically comfortable cat, simply because he is putting less weight on the affected joints.

In order to definitively diagnose any type of arthritis, your cat's vet will begin by observing your cat in movement and at rest, manipulating your cat's joints, and, ultimately, X-raying your cat.

If your vet does diagnose arthritis, he or she will probably recommend that you put your cat on a regimen of supplements, such as glucosamine and chondroitin, as well as modifying your cat's environment so that it's easier for him to get around. And your vet will definitely encourage you to put your cat on a weight-reducing diet.

Skin disorders. When a cat becomes overweight, it frequently becomes difficult for him to groom himself. Areas of his fur may become dirty, matted, and damp, which attracts lice or maggots.

If your cat is infested with lice, treatment is fairly simple: give your cat a thorough bath, followed by an insecticide. Follow up with diligent grooming.

When a cat becomes a host for maggots, treatment can be somewhat complex, depending on the severity of the infestation. When maggots nest in a cat, they literally punch holds in the cat's skin,

which may result in a bacterial infection. If the maggot infestation is severe enough, the cat could go into shock from toxins and enzymes secreted by the maggots. Treatment can include clipping, an insecticide-based shampoo, and an oral antibiotic.

Most cats object to being weighed, unlike Sue Gilsdorf's Little Tazzie.

HOW TO TELL IF YOUR CAT IS REALLY FAT

If you're not sure your cat has really gained weight, one of the best assessment tools are old pictures of your cat, preferably when he was around age one. They'll provide an accurate mirror of what your cat used to look like. Old videotapes provide even more information, showing you how your cat used to look and move.

Another thing to assess is your cat's energy level. Does he move and jump the way he used to? It's easy to lose track, especially if you've gotten too busy to really notice. (In fact, you may find that one of the side benefits of evaluating your cat's eating and exercise patterns may be an improvement in your own. A recent diet and exercise study put dogs and their owners on an exercise and weight loss program, with a very high level of success for both the pets and the people. While it's doubtful that cats would be quite so amenable, it does suggest that, as with human weight loss, partners and support groups really improve your chances for success.)

Eventually, hard numbers are what will help you tell the truth about your tabby. Check your cat's medical records. If your cat was at a healthy weight at age one, that's probably the weight to target.

To date, there is no such thing as a BMI for your cat, where you can assess your cat's build, muscle density, and percentage of fat and come out with an ideal weight target. Vets are still working with visual and tactile information when it comes to establishing goal weights for both dogs and cats.

The Internet provides a number of places where you can look at standards for cat sizes, from veterinary Web sites to pet food home pages. You can find sample pictures to illustrate the standard pet-weight labels, from emaciated to very obese, as well as dynamic assessment quizzes about your cat's current weight, feeding schedule, and activity level. Here's a helpful sample of sites:

www.iams.com
Features an animated "nutrition fact book" that shows how cats at different stages of life use nutrients in their food, as well as an animation where you can turn a fat cat into a thin cat and vice versa…by moving your (computer) mouse.

www.placervillevet.com/feline%20body%20condition.htm
This veterinary Web site contains both visual and verbal descriptions of cat body types.

To really get a sense of your cat's weight, you have to do two things: examine him and weigh him.

Stand over your cat while he, too, is standing, and get a good look at his back, his waist, and his hindquarters. A trim and healthy cat should have a defined waistline, an indentation that distinguishes it from his back and his hindquarters. Then, pick your cat up and feel for

his ribs. You should be able to feel them, and, ideally, count them individually, while feeling a little flesh at the same time. If all you can feel is flesh, and can't locate the ribs, then clearly your cat has a weight problem. (If your cat is too lean, with ribs visible to the last detail, that may signal another health issue, such as hyperthyroidism, which is often treated with radiation or surgery. To be absolutely sure, make sure you take your skinny cat to the vet for a complete checkup.)

Now, weigh your cat. All it takes is a regular scale, and a willingness to weigh yourself first. Step on the scale and get an adequate reading of your own weight. Step off. Then pick up your cat, and step on the scales again. Take the number. The different between your weight and that number is your cat's weight.

If for some reason, your cat has developed an aversion to being in the bathroom, or being anywhere near the bathroom scales, you have a couple of choices. You can use a baby scale, which a cat may prefer. Or you can weigh your cat's crate or cage on a regular scale. Then put your cat in the crate and weigh it all together. Use the same subtraction system. If your cat absolutely refuses, wait until you take him to the vet, and let the vet do it.

If you've determined that your cat is overweight, it may take some getting used to. And it's easy to feel that there are some very legitimate reasons for your cat's excess avoirdupois. But mostly, they're myths.

KITTY MYTHS AND TABBY TRUTHS

Even after you've accepted the fact that your cat is too heavy, you may feel that there's no way your cat is ever going to lose weight. The good news is most cats can and do lose weight. But to do it right, you need to debunk some of the following myths. The truth will set you on the road to better health for your cat.

Here are some common myths about cat obesity:

Myth: Indoor cats can't be fit; my apartment just isn't big enough for my cat to really get the exercise he needs.

Truth: Cats that have the run of a house—or an outdoor enclosure—do have more opportunities to scamper, and a 1997 Cornell University study revealed that cats with more room to move also tended to weigh less: the average house cat with three floors to frisk on will likely be slimmer than a studio apartment cat. But that doesn't mean you can't structure vigorous indoor playtime for your studio apartment cat. One very important thing to remember is that, unlike you, most cats (if they aren't too fat) can use more of your available surfaces than you can. Think Spiderman, or, well, Catwoman. In addition to getting your cat a cat tree where he can leap and scratch to his heart's content, you might even want to consider building a few shelves, or, short of that, choosing a surface or two that he's allowed to jump up on, and (just as exciting) stare out the window.

On the other hand, there are places a cat should NEVER play. They include the dishwasher, washing machine, clothes dryer, oven, or microwave, which should always be kept closed when you are not using them. Or, to quote Alice Rhea in her book *Good Cats, Bad Habits*, "No appliance should be started until you are sure it does not contain a cat."

Myth: My cat was spayed or neutered, so he's bound to put on poundage.

Truth: There is some truth to this myth. According to a 1997 study at Cornell, spayed or neutered cats were among the groups of felines most likely to be overweight or obese, at a rate of 3.4 times the rate of sexually intact cats. However, the average weight gain, likely caused by the loss of the androgenic hormones estrogen and testosterone, is usually a matter of ounces. Be aware that, if you haven't spayed or neutered your cat because of this concern, you are also putting your cat at risk for several serious health issues—sexually intact female cats are far more likely to get breast cancer, for instance, while female cats spayed before puberty avoid ovarian and uterine cancer entirely. Male cats who haven't been neutered roam their territory and mark everywhere. The goal should be to keep your cat healthy, and that means spaying or neutering your cat, and then watching his or her calorie intake.

Myth: My cat is old, and you just can't teach an old cat new tricks, especially in the areas of diet and exercise.

Truth: No question about it: Cats are very, very fond of routine, and as they age, they typically love it even more. Most cats, frankly, are not crazy about it when you put them on a diet, and in the beginning, they are going to let you know about it.

But, as with humans, the key to any weight loss program is patient persistence. Take baby steps, and go easy on your old cat. (While cats do age at different speeds, depending on their health histories, a typical 12-year-old cat is about 65 in human years.) Should older cats lose weight more slowly than young cats? Absolutely. And unlike dogs, who sometimes profit from a couple days' complete fast from food, cats should never be put on a fast. Put your cat on a crash diet, and you may put him at risk for a potentially fatal liver disease, hepatic lipidosis.

The exact cause of hepatic lipidosis is unknown, but the result is frequently fatal. A cat suffering from hepatic lipidosis usually goes on a "hunger strike" lasting from days to weeks, which causes fat to accumulate in the liver, frequently leading to jaundice, and then to liver failure. If the condition is caught early enough, the cat can recover via a stringent treatment regimen, including fluid replacement, forced feeding, and possibly a surgically inserted feeding tube. An older cat is less likely to survive both the disease and the cure.

Does that mean an older cat can't lose weight? No. It simply means that you want to change his diet and up his exercise quotient very slowly; much more slowly than what you would put yourself or a younger cat through. But remind yourself when the going gets rough that a successful weight loss plan will give you many extra healthy days with your senior cat. Statistics tell us that the average indoor cat will now live into his early teens, and many live to a ripe old age of 20+ years. Let them be good fit years.

Myth: I don't have time to get my cat thin.

Truth: If you're a typical pet owner, this probably is your number one excuse—and it's a serious one. Despite the cat's low-maintenance reputation, caring for any kind of an animal still takes time, and it may feel as if it's time that you don't have. But given the long-term impact weight has on your cat's health, you may eventually be spending time, and lots of it, taking your cat to the vet and dealing with weight-related illnesses.

Myth: My cat isn't fat, he's just big-boned.

Truth: This is a myth so popular, it's the name of a popular book of cartoons. It is true that not all cats are born the same, and while there is less size variation in cats than in dogs, you will never mistake a petite hair-less sphinx for a Maine Coon. Some breeds do grow larger than others.

Here are some typical healthy weights for adult purebred cats. Typically, female cats weigh less than male cats, so the range can be wide.

Your Cat's Weight in Pounds	
Abyssinian	9–17 pounds
American or European Burmese	8–14 pounds
American shorthair	8–15 pounds
Cornish Rex	6–10 pounds
Devon Rex	6–9 pounds
Egyptian Mau	5–11 pounds
Exotic shorthair	7–14 pounds
Maine Coon	9–22 pounds
Manx	8–12 pounds
Ocicat	6–14 pounds
Persian	8–15 pounds
Ragdoll	10–20 pounds
Scottish fold	6–13 pounds
Siamese	6–12 pounds

As you can see, weights can vary widely among breeds. But no breed ought to have a stomach like Fred Flintstone. And while it's unlikely that you'll be reported to the authorities for overfeeding your cat in America, in other countries, things can be a little tougher. Recently, a 41-pound cat in Germany was removed from his owner's home and put in a shelter—not to be given up for adoption, but to reeducate the cat in the ways of normal eating.

With some breeds of cat, it is quite easy to tell when a cat has gained a few. Other breeds have the luxury of hiding their avoirdupois under a luxurious coat. Dr. Emily Levine, D.V.M., who actually put 60 fat cats on a diet during a Cornell research project in 2004, admits that some cats hide their fat better than others, thanks to abundant fur, a forgiving body type, or both. The only way to establish whether these cats had gained or lost weight was to weigh them on a scale that was calibrated to both pounds and ounces. But there isn't that much variation. Unlike dogs, cats have a reasonably uniform size and shape, usually weighing between 6 and 12 pounds. A larger breed cat usually tops out at around 20 pounds. Just because your cat "carries" his excess weight well doesn't mean he's doing well.

Myth: My cat is just naturally lazy. It's the breed.

Truth: There is no question that there are "fast cats" and "slow cats," just as some people naturally prefer a sprint to a leisurely park stroll. In the animal world Olympics, cats are sprinters, not marathoners. There's a natural tendency to assume that just because your cat doesn't move much, he doesn't like to move at all.

If your cat is seriously overweight, he may have become less active to compensate for his extra pounds. He may even be unable to jump, and both his heart and his lungs are working overtime. He may not be lazy so much as suffering under the strain.

If this isn't the case, think about this: have you been training your cat to be lazy? Have you been sending her signals that suggest that it's better to stay put and get fed than to run around and work for her supper? While the history of cat training is a lot shorter than that of dog training, it exists. The growth of both cat agility and clicker training for cats (covered later on in this book) prove that cats not only can be trained to be active—they actually come to crave it.

Even if you don't want to have your cat jump through hoops (though you could!) you have a lot more influence over your cat's activity level than you realize. Pick up your cat's favorite toy, or, even better, a little dry kibble, and tempt your cat to follow you. Then skip down the hallway. Chances are very good that your "lazy" cat will follow you wherever you go. It may also be that your home is not set up to be cat exercise friendly. Some cats don't like to move around until night time. Some cats adore scaling heights, and leaping from point to point. Making some simple adjustments in your home, such as installing a cat tree, or providing a perch on a window sill (preferably near a bird feeder) may change your cat's activity level dramatically.

Getting your cat slim may also mean a positive personality change. Unlike dogs, cats remain quite close in breeding and behavior to their wilder cousins, who travel many miles to hunt down their food. That spirit and breeding are still in your fat cat. Think of it this way: Helping your fat cat move more and eat less isn't just about health—it's about returning your feline to his natural state of magnificence.

HOW TO USE THIS BOOK

The first step to using this book is making sure that you have a genuinely healthy cat, and that starts out with a visit to the vet and a complete checkup. The second step to using this book is to have patience. Remember: Helping your cat lose weight will take time—but not as much time as you think. According to human research, nearly any program of self-improvement begins with bumps and false starts, rarely a straight line. People rarely get it the first time—it's just not the way we're wired. Since you are effectively becoming your cat's diet and exercise coach, remember to be gentle both with your cat and with yourself. Keep the bar low and the expectations minimal at first, so as to keep success possible. Your cat's progress will be measured in ounces and half ounces.

Putting your cat on a diet may bring up some uncomfortable issues about your own health. However, keep in mind that you are your cat's primary caretaker, and in fact may succeed better and faster with your cat than you have with yourself. As your cat's caretaker, you have extraordinary control over what your cat eats, and how much he moves. You may actually make a psychological shift as you help your cat slenderize, and begin to take a more assertive role in your own care and feeding.

WHO ISN'T THIS BOOK FOR?

This book is not for you if your cat currently suffers from other serious health issues, such as diabetes, hypothyroidism, or any other metabolically related issues. It cannot be stressed strongly enough: if you know or even suspect that your fat cat is suffering from an illness, run, do not walk to your vet, and get a complete physical.

The purpose of this book is simple: to give you, the caring cat owner, basic, easy-to-use tools to help your fat cat lose weight—or to keep your slim cat on an

Long after Leia has outgrown this basket, it is still her favorite spot to nap.

even keel. The book will deal with some of the common kitty myths, as well as introduce you to some new ways to keep your cat in great shape. For instance, is it really true that an outdoor cat is healthier than an indoor cat? Can adding a second cat help your fat cat lose weight? What's the deal with the Atkins diet?

If you are a modern pet owner, it's likely you feel you don't have enough time to take care of your own health, let alone your cat's. So, start with just a minute. This book offers "Fat Minutes"—short tests, exercises, and helpful information you can read quickly that will move your cat further along the path of health and well-being. When you feel like you don't have time to read a chapter, flip to a Fat Minute—and give it a try. Turn the page for your first Fat Minute.

Five Fat Minutes: The Fat Cat Log

It's a basic of human weight loss: Keeping track of what and how much you eat and move seems to automatically help the weight loss process. Unfortunately, cats can't write down what they eat or how much they run. So that's your job. You can also use this log to have more informed conversations with your vet.

The Fat Cat Log is divided into three sections: Food, Activity, and Tracking/Training.

Food is pretty self-evident, but it's vital to keep track of ALL the food your cat consumes, not just what you give him. If your cat is fat and you have already been keeping a stringent eye on his intake, it's likely somebody else is overfeeding your feline.

Activity means quality of movement, as well as quantity. How long is your cat playing, and with what, and with whom? What kind of energy does your cat have?

Training/Tracking: It is one of the great cat myths that your cat can't or won't be trained, but a myth is exactly what it is. In other chapters, we'll discuss how exactly training can help your fat cat have more fun—and how you can bring more pleasure to the cat/human bond. The truth is you're training your cat even when you're doing nothing. So keep track of that nothing until you decide to change it. You'll probably find that you do expect your cat to do certain things and that you do actually offer rewards for behavior—you just haven't been conscious about doing it.

Copy the Fat Cat Log, and use it for at least three days. You'll be surprised at how much you learn about your cat.

Sample Fat Cat Log

FOOD

Today I fed my cat: 2 times

I chose to feed my cat _____ ad lib (or free feeding) or __X__ fixed times

Name of food(s): dry lamb meat and rice weight control fomula

Total amount: 3/4 cups   0 cans

Number of snacks: 2 tuna treats

Water consumption: 8 oz.

Any additional food or snacks?
not today

ACTIVITY

Number of play sessions: 3

Total duration of play sessions: 25 minutes

Toys: feather on a stick, catnip mouse

Activity partners: I played with her for one of her sessions

On a scale of 1 to 10, 10 being most active, my cat's activity level was: 6

TRAINING AND TRACKING

Tomorrow, in order to make my cat healthier, I plan to:
purchase a clicker and begin training my cat to do a trick for dinner

In a month, it would be great if my cat would:
be able to jump on the windowsill like she used to

My cat seems to really like:
when I play with her, she seems more inclined to be active

Your Fat Cat Log

FOOD

Today I fed my cat: _____

I chose to feed my cat ____ ad lib (or free feeding) or _____ fixed times

Name of food(s): _____

Total amount: _____ cups _____ cans

Number of snacks: _____

Water consumption: _____ oz.

Any additional food or snacks?

_____

ACTIVITY

Number of play sessions: _____

Total duration of play sessions: _____

Toys: _____

Activity partners: _____

On a scale of 1 to 10, 10 being most active, my cat's activity level was: ____

TRAINING AND TRACKING

Tomorrow, in order to make my cat healthier, I plan to:

_____

In a month, it would be great if my cat would:

_____

My cat seems to really like:

_____

SUMMARY

- If your cat is in good health, it is possible for him to lose weight be decreasing calories and increasing activity.
- While there are guidelines for what a healthy cat looks like, the bottom line is that you must weigh your cat to the ounce to determine if your cat is at a healthy weight.
- Before beginning your cat's diet, make sure that you take him in for a check-up.
- Before taking your cat to the vet, begin a log of your cat's food consumption and activity to get a true picture of your cat's health.

Prepare for Your Vet Visit

When is a good time to ask your vet about slimming down your fat cat? Ideally, it's before your cat is fat—or even before he becomes a full-grown cat, when he's still a lithe, fluffy kitten. Prevention is 9/10 of the weight loss game, for cats as well as humans. It's important to realize that small choices and subtle changes to your kitten's food and play patterns could have a lifetime impact on his health and longevity.

However, it's likely, if you're reading this book, that your cat is no kitty, and it's definitely time to begin your cat's diet. Go to your vet armed with information, and be ready with questions. And be prepared for the vet to ask a few of his own.

BEFORE YOU VISIT THE VET

Before you visit the vet, make a list of what you know about your cat's eating and exercise habits. You can either use the Fat Cat Log in the first chapter of the book, or carry a pocket notebook around with you and write down exactly what your cat eats and drinks for three days. Briefly summarize what kind of exercise your cat likes—plays alone, plays with others, or plays outside, and how long each play session lasts.

Take note of any recent activity or diet changes. While your fat cat has probably just had too many calories and too little movement, it's possible that his weight gain is due to other health issues and your log can help you pinpoint what those may be. Along the way, you'll probably learn something about your cat. And by the time you visit the vet, you'll already be planning an active attack on your cat's fat.

If you're feeling anxious about approaching your vet, remember: your vet wants to help. Your vet is an animal lover like you, and may even be the owner of a chubby cat or fat dog herself. Dr. Jennifer Jellison, D.V.M., a practicing vet in Columbus, Ohio, admits she is no stranger to fat pets, or the struggle to keep them healthy. Her Labrador retriever carries 30 extra pounds. "I have a retired service dog that can open the refrigerator," she confesses. When counseling owners of overweight pets, she always lets them know this; she's been where they've been, and she knows it isn't easy.

QUESTIONS FOR YOUR VET

With that in mind, go to the vet's office prepared to make your vet your partner in healthy cat weight loss. After making sure your cat is in good health, make sure that you get a chance to ask your vet the following questions:

How much does my cat weigh?

Make sure you learn your cat's weight in pounds and ounces. Successful weight loss in cats is measured in ounces per week, not pounds. The more precise your measurements, the more likely you are to keep track of and promote your cat's weight loss.

How much weight should my cat lose?
How long will it take?

This weight goal will be as individual as your cat. Because there is no standard such as the BMI (Body Mass Index) for cats or dogs, it's especially important to ask your vet, who will have seen many more types of cats, what your cat's target weight should be. Your vet should tell you that the weight loss process should be slow and steady. He should also warn you that if the cat becomes finicky and refuses to eat while on a diet for more than two days, then the cat could be in serious medical crisis, and should be taken immediately to an emergency facility. A cat who puts himself on a starvation diet is a cat headed for trouble.

Does my cat need a special diet food?

If your cat has other health issues, he may already be on a prescription cat food, and generally, it isn't recommended that he come off it and switch to a diet food. While some vets may recommend specific pet foods, few suggest that it's the only way to go. Current research indicates that as long as a cat is being fed a restricted but adequate amount of a nutritionally complete food, he will lose weight—whether the food is high protein, low-fat, organic, or some combination thereof.

Discuss with your vet if there are any particular advantages to a cat food he recommends, but keep an open mind.

The one special diet you can't put your cat on is vegetarian. Cats are carnivores, designed to eat animal protein. While they can and do eat vegetables, and fiber, they cannot subsist on this. They must have animal protein.

Do I really need to spay/neuter my cat?

There's really no debate about this. Unless you are a cat breeder, you must spay or neuter your cat for the good of the cat, and the world around him or her. The fantasy remains that a sexually intact cat is a happier cat. The facts don't support it. Cats in heat spray, fight, and generally stink up the house. Spaying and neutering should be done at about six months of age, before the average cat reaches puberty. (During spring mating season, or in multicat households, a female can, occasionally, mature earlier. Depending on their breed, some cats do mature earlier or later than that, but six months is a good time to get in touch with your vet to discuss the issue.) If you adopt a sexually intact adult cat, it is still important to schedule him or her for spaying or neutering. Spaying or neutering your adult cats reduces their chances of contracting some forms of cancer, infections, and sexually transmitted diseases, as well as making them calmer, more stable felines.

Will my cat need drugs?

If you or your vet suspect your cat has metabolic issues, the only way your vet can establish this is through a series of tests. In the case of diabetes, thyroid diseases, or other metabolically-related health issues, drugs are often a likely component to treating your fat cat. Typical treatments of cats with diabetes include administering insulin, for example.

But the vast majority of fat cats are not suffering from a serious disease; they simply have too much food and too little exercise. And that's actually good news. It means that as an owner you probably have all the tools necessary to help your cat get healthy. If you get your cat slim now, it's likely that later on, he will evade any number of diseases aggravated by obesity.

QUESTIONS YOUR VET WANTS YOU TO ANSWER

While your vet may not have the time to play pet diet detective, providing him with the following answers will help you both to slim down your cat. The following are things your vet may want to ask you.

Have you noticed any changes in your cat's feeding or activity patterns?

Changes in these areas can be the tip-off to other health issues, from joint problems to diabetes. Even if it turns out that your cat is normal, it's important to have a conversation with your vet about what "normal" activity and eating look like, so that you're in agreement.

Do you measure your cat's food?
Do you know how much a cup of food is?

This is another part of establishing what "normal" looks like. Many well-meaning cat lovers, Dr. Emily Levine reports, never measure

See the vet long before your cat hits the 29-pound mark.

their cat's food, and grossly overestimate the amount the cat actually needs. During an exam, Dr. Jellison actually takes out a cup measure and pours out a cup of dry food. That is a whole day's worth of food for an average cat weighing between 7 and 9 pounds.

Who else feeds your cat?

Dr. Martha Gearhart, D.V.M., of the Pleasant Valley Animal Hospital of Pleasant Valley, New York, reports that well-meaning pet owners can be sabotaged by "the others," meaning friends, family members, and, in the case of outdoor cats, both neighbors and the outside (cat snack-filled) world. A vet visit can be the perfect time to assess just who else might be stuffing your cat full of treats. Discussing this with the vet gives you the opportunity to begin an action plan to convince the others to help you slim down your cat.

Who else takes care of your cat?

You may believe that when you leave your cat at home with family members, your cat scampers and plays. The reality may be something closer to this: Your well-meaning caretaker sits in a chair, watches television, and likes to feed the cat all day because it keeps the cat near. Successful weight loss in a pet involves identifying all the factors and all the people who contribute to your cat's weight gain, and enlisting them in the campaign for change. This may not happen overnight, but it can happen.

Are you ready to change?

Dr. Martha Gearhart admits that the first thing she does when discussing a cat's weight problem is look at the owner. If the cat is fat and the owner is of average size, she says, then it's generally easy to enlist the owner. Dr. Jellison, though, has noted that in her practice, nearly all cat owners, regardless of size, focus intently on their cats' ups and downs in weight.

In fact, there is growing evidence that pet owners are ready, even anxious, to help their cats lose weight. Dr. Levine conducted a Cornell University study last year that put 60 obese cats on a weight loss regimen. While searching for participants, Dr. Levine learned that news of the study somehow got distributed nationally. The result? Her study received "hundreds of calls" from cat owners all over the U.S. anxious to enroll their cats in the diet program. Regretfully, she had to turn down all but the local applicants.

But however motivated you are, remember changing your cat's eating and exercise habits will cause short-term stress. Cats aren't any crazier about diets than humans are. But there are ways to cope in the chapters to follow.

SUMMARY

- Enlist your vet directly to help you establish exactly what might be causing your cat's excess weight.
- Most overweight cats are normal, healthy cats who eat too much and move too little, who can lose weight on a balanced, calorie-restricted diet.
- Work with your vet to establish realistic weight loss targets.

Rule Out Other Health Problems

Is it possible that your fat cat's weight has causes other than lack of exercise and overeating?

It is unlikely, but not impossible. As noted in Chapter 2, your Fat Cat Log and a visit to the vet will usually tell you if one of the following comparatively rare medical conditions may be to blame for your cat's excess weight.

PREGNANCY

Because there is no pregnancy test for cats as there is for people, it can be difficult to tell in the earliest stages whether your cat is pregnant, going through a false pregnancy, or simply gaining weight. Some pregnant cats actually experience listlessness and go through morning sickness in early pregnancy. Midway through a typical pregnancy (about 35 days), a pregnant cat's nipples will turn pink, and her belly will enlarge further.

To determine whether your cat is carrying kittens, a vet can use abdominal ultrasound early in the pregnancy, and abdominal X-rays in the latter stages of the pregnancy. In the early stages of your cat's pregnancy, a vet can also carefully palpate (examine by touch) the cat's belly to locate the position of the kittens. In the latter stages, the kittens' movements may actually ripple their mother's belly.

FALSE PREGNANCY

A sexually intact female cat experiences a false pregnancy when ovulation occurs, but the eggs remain unfertilized. Cats going through false pregnancies show many of the same signs as a genuine pregnancy, including increased appetite, weight gain, and even nesting behavior. On rare occasions, they will even produce milk. The condition, which is not dangerous, usually passes in a matter of weeks.

HYPOTHYROIDISM

Your cat's metabolism is controlled by his thyroid gland, two lobes found near his larynx. When his thyroid gland underproduces thyroid hormones, the metabolism slows down.

A cat suffering from hypothyroidism displays a variety of symptoms in addition to being overweight. Typically, he moves lethargically, and seems almost "zonked out." He may overgroom; his fur is frequently dull and patchy. (In contrast, a healthy overweight cat looks fat and happy—his coat is shiny, he moves well, and he is alert to the world around him.)

Hypothyroidism is diagnosed by administering a thyroid blood test. Treatment involves administering an oral thyroid supplement once or twice daily. Typically, cats begin to lose weight in two to four weeks.

Hypothyroidism is a very rare condition in cats. Cats are far more likely to suffer from an overactive thyroid, known as hyperthyroidism, where a cat loses weight rapidly.

BLOAT

All of sudden, seemingly overnight, your cat's belly appears to swell. The cause could be anything from a couple of days of food indulgence to a very serious heart condition. Better to be safe than sorry: if you notice a significant change in your cat's abdomen, take him to the vet immediately.

The leading causes of temporary bloat in adult cats are overeating, eating fermented foods, and constipation. All of these conditions can be treated fairly easily by changing the cat's diet, and are not generally life-threatening.

However, if your cat's belly doesn't flatten out following a diet change, or his stomach swells suddenly and he appears to be in pain, the cause could be a bowel obstruction, bladder outlet obstruction, abscessed uterus (a life-threatening bacterial infection seen most often in sexually intact females over the age of five), or peritonitis (an almost uniformly lethal, but rare, viral infection). In all of these cases, if your cat is both bloated and in pain, rush your cat to the veterinary hospital. These are medical emergencies.

Other forms of illness related to bloating may develop over a series of days or weeks, and they also require medical attention. Gradual

Elvis, a diabetic cat, spends much of his time lounging around and gets very little exercise.

swelling of your cat's abdomen could indicate one of the following conditions: ascites (a fluid accumulation in the abdomen, indicating feline infectious peritonitis), right-sided heart failure (in contrast to left-sided heart failure, which generally causes lung congestion), or liver disease.

To definitively diagnose any of these conditions, you must take your cat to the vet. The good news is that if you are already monitoring your cat's body type, eating, and exercise, you're in much better position to notice when there's something "off" about your cat's tummy. Take it seriously.

SUMMARY

- Enlist your vet directly to help you establish exactly what might be causing your cat's excess weight.
- Most overweight cats are normal, healthy cats who eat too much and move too little, who can lose weight on a balanced, calorie-restricted diet.
- Work with your vet to establish realistic weight loss targets.

Learn What to Feed Your Cat

The number one reason your cat got fat is simple: He ate too much. It's understandable. Like humans, cats spent thousands of years hunting for their food, often traveling several miles a day to eat a few mice, if they were lucky. Even in ancient Egypt, where cats were worshipped as gods, they still had to pull their weight by hunting mice in the royal palace. But most modern cats have lost their jobs, as well as their mobility, while acquiring, through you, an almost unlimited access to food. How do you meet your cat's need for sustenance, his body's nutritional requirements, and keep your sanity at the same time? This chapter will outline the building blocks of a healthy cat's diet, what to look for on a cat food label, and what's actually in a diet cat food.

CATS: THE ORIGINAL MEAT EATERS

The current fear of carbs has reached the animal kingdom, and it is not uncommon to hear a pet owner say, "I'm Atkins-ing my cat." In fact, a cat Atkins diet actually reflects what your cat might have eaten in the wild. Unlike dogs, who ate whatever they could get (the technical term being omnivores), cats got the vast amount of their nutrients from animal protein, which usually meant rodents or birds, and their metabolisms adjusted to that. In scientific terms, they are known as obligate carnivores. To survive, a cat must consume animal protein. While cats do, in fact, need carbohydrates in very limited doses (mice and rats usually contained small amounts of grain and grass), he cannot be a vegetarian, no matter how much you might wish it.

Getting a clear picture of what you feed your cat is the first step to a successful cat diet plan. But how do you know what's good for your cat?

WHO'S WATCHING OUT FOR MY CAT'S FOOD?

In the beginning the only judge of what was tasty was the cat himself. Now, cat food is overseen by a voluntary regulatory body, the Association of American Feed Control Officials (AAFCO). AAFCO sets the nutritional standards that you see on cat food labels. Currently, AAFCO offers two ways to "pass" their standard, and one is preferable to the other.

The first way is based on a purely chemical analysis of the nutrients in your cat's food. Some joke that, using this standard, a shoe filled with motor oil could meet the AAFCO chemical standards. While it's a joke, it's true that the chemical standard does not require that the source of the food be of high quality.

The second preferred AAFCO standard is based on feeding trials with real live cats. To pass the feeding trials, manufacturers feed their products to cats to assure that the products maintain feline good health. This is a more "real world" test, and definitely the one you should be looking for when shopping for cat food.

However, this standard is far from perfect. Feeding trials are of a short duration, typically six months. The ideal food trial, some say, would last two years and span two complete generations of cats, in order to certify that the food was appropriate and healthy throughout a cat's lifespan. This is an expensive and time-consuming process which most companies have not yet adopted.

One Fat Minute: Taste Bud Truths

The typical human possesses about 9,000 taste buds.

The typical dog boasts 1700.

The typical cat? Only 470. However, what cats lack in number, they make up in focus. Cats' taste buds are unusually attuned to the taste of flesh.

There's a very good reason to choose commercially-produced cat food for your furry friend. It's convenient, and it's consistent. Assuming that you have checked the labels, you can be reasonably sure that what you're giving your cat is what he'll be eating. In order to represent its product as "complete," "balanced," "perfect," "scientific," "for all life stages," or "formulated for growth, pregnancy, or lactation," a company must adhere to specific AAFCO standards.

But it's impossible to ignore the controversy, and the growing literature, that deals with the idea that the best diet for your cat is a more "natural" one. Just what does that mean?

The controversy embraces a number of issues. Current standards are broad enough so that protein in cat food, for instance, can come from high-quality, human-grade organic chicken—or meat by-products, poultry by-products (including beaks and claws), fish by-products, soybean meals, and cereal grains, which may lack both quality and digestibility.

Another issue is the labeling loophole that allows a cat food label to list an appealing ingredient such as "beef," or "chicken," while the food itself contains as little as 3% of the item listed. Yet another popular criticism is of the various food processing methods used to create cat food, which can diminish the food sources' original nutritional value.

Many smaller, "natural" pet food companies have sprung up in the midst of this heated controversy. For example, the founders of the Blue Buffalo Company of Wilton, Connecticut, were inspired by the fight against cancer that CEO Bill Bishop's Airedale, Blue, went through—three times. The search for high quality ingredients to help maintain Blue's health led to the creation of Blue Buffalo, a cat and dog food company advised by Dr. Bob Goldstein, D.V.M., a holistic vet based in Westport, Connecticut, Medical Director of the Healing Center for Animals, and developer of a nutritional blood test for animals. Blue Buffalo's food is made up of variety of natural ingredients, and processed in a way that its founders feel that the food retains more of its nutrients. The top two ingredients in their Cat Life Protection Formula are a very healthy portion of protein in the form of human-grade deboned chicken and chicken meal, and also in the top ten, brown rice, whole carrots, and whole sweet potatoes.

If you're worried about the source of your cat's chow, foods from smaller, more independent companies may be the way to go, especially when you're concerned about the quality of the calories your cat is consuming. To find out just what kind of testing your cat food has undergone, always start with the label. Some companies describe precisely what kind of testing they've performed on their foods. If that's not available, call them up and ask them. You owe it to your cat.

The Pet Food Institute, the trade association of pet food manufacturers, offers an online guide to translating pet food labels, which can be found at www.petfoodreport.com. The Web site walks the viewer through different fictional types of pet food, depending on the age, health, and species of pet, and explains what the somewhat mysterious list of ingredients means.

The bottom line, regardless of the brand you ultimately choose, is to make sure that the label assures you that the food provides "Complete and Balanced Nutrition." If you are feeding a kitten, make sure that the label includes the term "for all life stages."

SO...WHAT SHOULD MY CAT'S FOOD CONTAIN? PORTRAIT OF A CAT'S DIET

Assuming that your cat is in good health, it may or may not be necessary to change his food. You may choose to cut the amount of your cat's current food up to 25%, while carefully monitoring how he responds to the diminished portions. However, if you do so, make sure that your fat cat's new diet ration meets his minimum daily nutritional requirements.

The perfect cat diet in the wild is simple: mice, mice, and more mice. Unfortunately, most cats don't have access to that many mice. But it's good to keep that image in mind when feeding your cat. Also, keep in mind the number 60. According to current research, the complete cat diet includes over 60 nutrients, which can be found in AAFCO-approved cat food, and should be your focus when designing your fat cat's diet. Here is a list of the most significant of those 60.

Protein. Protein is vital for healthy cat nutrition, and the typical cat needs it in much higher percentages than we humans do. As a species, cats need more protein than any other domesticated species, and uses the protein consumed to get vital amino acids. A good cat diet should contain between 26–35% crude protein on a dry matter basis (check the label to be sure).

Fat. Fat should be reduced, not eliminated, in a cat's diet plan. Fat delivers vital fat-soluble vitamins such as A, D, E, and K, and essential fatty acids they cannot manufacture in their own bodies. Check your cat's food label to make sure he's receiving between 7–14% of dry matter.

Carbohydrates. Carbohydrates are not something cats seek out in the wild (though they will find some in the grasses they chew or in feed inside the mice they eat). Cats do use carbohydrates for fuel. In most commercial cat foods, carbohydrates make up the largest single component.

Vitamins. Vitamin deficiencies are rare in cats that are eating a commercial diet. Those who are making food for their cats from scratch need to be especially aware of these requirements. Vitamins A and D: Unlike other animals, cats cannot naturally synthesize these vitamins, so they must be included in their diet. Vitamin B complex are required for healthy cats in high doses, and supplements are frequently prescribed for sick cats. Vitamins E and K are often given to those cats suffering from liver disease. They usually receive these vitamins as supplements. Underweight cats also benefit from extra E and K.

Amino acids. Amino acids are a vital part of your cat's nutritional package; cats require 13 in all to have a balanced diet. The most newsworthy amino acid as far as cats are concerned is taurine. Since the discovery in the 1980s that inadequate taurine in cat diet led to a heart disease known as dilated cardiomyopathy, cat food manufacturers have changed their formulas so that any typical off-the-shelf cat food includes a healthy amount. (This is also why it is important to be aware of supplements if you decide to make your cat's food yourself; taurine does not naturally occur in the foods you are most likely to be feeding your cat.)

Minerals. Another long-term investment in the health of your cat's teeth is making sure he's getting enough calcium and phosphorous, both important minerals that help maintain a cat's dental health.

Water. Did you know that your cat is between 60 and 70 percent water? The average indoor cat needs approximately eight ounces of water a day. Cats who exclusively eat dry food need more; canned food cats, generally less. And while water usually gets less of your cat's attention than his almighty food, it's something that affects his health.

CAT FOOD TYPES

Cat food comes in three distinct types: dry, canned, and semimoist. It is the processing that makes these foods look so different from each other.

Dry food, or kibble, is made up of a cereal-based food mixed with meat or dairy products. It is made in a machine called an extruder, the same machine that makes breakfast cereal. An extruder combines the processes of a meat grinder with a pressure cooker. In the food's final cooking stages, it is sprayed with fat and flavors before it is dried and packaged.

Semimoist food uses a variety of protein sources, such as fish, beef, liver, and chicken. It is created using a principle called intermediate moisture technology. The food stays soft because of higher levels of water. Added preservatives prevent spoilage. When semimoist food is put through an extruder, it can be shaped into a variety of forms—even made to look like a marbled piece of meat.

Canned food, made up of meat, fish, and vegetable sources, is processed much in the same way food is canned at home. The meat is first ground fine and then mixed with water. Dry ingredients, including vitamins, are added, and then the mixture is put in a can. After the lid is applied to the can, the can goes into a type of pressure cooker for 50 to 90 minutes.

So what are typical nutrient and calorie counts for each type of food? According to *The Cat Owner's Veterinary Handbook,* it looks like this:

Dry: 34% protein, 12% fat, 105 calories per ounce

Semi-moist: 36% protein, 17% fat, 75 calories per ounce

Canned: 41% protein, 14% fat, 29 calories per ounce

WHAT IS DIET FOOD AND DOES MY CAT NEED IT?

Cat food manufacturers have responded to the spike in cat obesity by providing a variety of cat foods that are generally labeled "low-fat" or "lite." (To qualify for the "lite" or "low-fat" labels, pet foods must meet specific AAFCO standards.) Some even offer "twofers," such as the Iams dry food that offers both weight and hairball control. According to the Iams website, which lists nutritional and calorie values for its foods, Indoor Weight & Hairball Care contains 303 calories per cup. Iams also offers Adult Weight Control, which is slightly higher in calories (346 per cup). Both diet formulas provide fewer calories than, for example, two of Iams' regular adult formulas, which vary from 433 calories per cup in the Original formula to 461 in the Lamb and Rice formula.

The two regular foods offer a slightly higher percentage of protein in food: not less than 32% vs. not less than 28% in the two diet foods. (This 'not less than' phrase also means that the food may have more of the nutrient listed; bear this in mind if you are trying to restrict any particular nutrient in your cat's diet.)

According to *The Humane Society of United States Complete Guide to Cat Care,* an adult cat needs at least 26% protein in his food, so all four foods are in the normal range. The four foods' nutritional listings, with the exception of higher fiber in the hairball formula, are virtually identical except for one element. Where the lite and regular foods diverge is in the percentage of fat: not less than 21% for the regular foods, and not less than 11% or more than 13.5% for the weight loss foods.

So is it worth it to make the switch to a diet food, if your cat's been used to a regular cat food formula? It depends. Based on the most recent research done by Dr. Emily Levine, cats who ate a high-fiber, low-fat cat food seemed to lose weight somewhat more easily than cats who ate a higher-fat, low-calorie cat food, or ate a regular cat food. However, over the course of the study, the type of food was not significant in the cat's weight loss. The key was calories. As long as a cat's calories were restricted, he lost weight.

So if your cat is currently happy with his food, and it's simply a problem of overfeeding, you might simply want to start measuring out a smaller portion, keeping in mind his nutritional requirements. If your cat really responds to the higher level of fat in the regular formulas, he may turn up his nose at a low-fat feed. However, some cats simply love to eat a lot of something, so switching to a lower-calorie food, but keeping the quantity constant, might be the solution.

Should you choose to really fine tune your cat's diet and do some serious comparison shopping, a good place to start is at the Feline Diabetes Web site's food pages:

www.felinediabetes.com/cat_food_nutrition_dry.htm
www.felinediabetes.com/cat_ food_nutrition_ canned.htm

Here, you'll find many brands of canned and dry cat foods analyzed by protein, fat, carbohydrates, fiber, phosphorus, and calories, with links to the companies' Web site.

HOW TO PICK THE RIGHT FOOD AT THE RIGHT TIME

The wealth of cat food on the shelves is enough to intimidate anyone, especially someone with a cat who's a little too hefty. Before you buy your next bag or can, make sure you've taken some basics into account.

How Old is My Cat?

Kittens between two and six months have twice the energy and nutrient needs of adult cats. Pick your food accordingly; buy a kitten-appropriate mix for your kitten until he is a year old. Then, begin the transition to adult cat food. (In a pinch, in a multi-cat household, it's perfectly appropriate to feed an older cat some kitten food—just keep in mind that the food is usually much higher in calories.)

One of the most important ways you can avoid making your cat fat is to feed him a healthy (but not overwhelming) variety of foods as a kitten, as soon as possible. Cats' bodies are physically flexible, but their palates tend to lock in quite early. By the time a cat celebrates his six-month birthday, his food preferences have settled. It's still possible to introduce new things, but it gets harder.

Senior cats (ten years and older) frequently need easy-to-chew, easy-to-digest, food—and less of it.

Does My Cat Have Any Special Needs?

Diabetes, kidney disease, immune system issues, even hairballs—all may be better managed with the right diet. Talk to your vet about whether a special vet-prescribed diet will help. Among the specialty cat food types currently available on the market are:

Oral Care

Hairball Relief

Sensitive Skin

Whether your cat's illness necessitates a change in diet is something to work out with your vet. However, here are some general rules of thumb: Cats with diabetes may benefit from a diet high in fat and protein and low in carbohydrates. Cats with colitis, constipation, or anal gland disease can often be helped by increased fiber in the diet. Cats with heart disease may need a special diet with decreased amounts of sodium and increased amounts of the amino acid taurine.

FOOD NO-NOS

While your cat is adjusting to his diet, he may choose to chew on some, or a lot, of other things in and out of the house. Unfortunately, many substances can wreak havoc on your cat's digestive system, ranging from mild stomach upset to death. Here are some of the likely offenders:

Milk. It's a cartoon fantasy that persists to this day: a little kitten lapping at a bowl of cow's milk. But the magic of kitties and cow milk

The Vegetarian Cat: An Urban Legend

If you're a vegetarian, no doubt you'd probably prefer if your cat was, too, but it is not to be. It's an admirable desire, but an unrealistic one. According to the most current research, cats still need a protein-rich meat source in order to function well. Some cats do learn to love vegetables, but while veggies clearly provide healthful nutrients, they can never be the core of a healthy cat's diet. Channel your enthusiasm for "natural" eating into finding the best and the freshest ingredients for your cat. There's no question that over many generations, a new kind of vegetarian cat might evolve, much as a dog's domestication probably led him to be an opportunistic eater of practically everything, but cats didn't walk down that evolutionary path. Inside your cat lives the same wild huntress who kept ancient Egypt mouse-free. Don't deny her identity.

is just a myth. Many cats are lactose intolerant, and suffer diarrhea from your well-meaning milk donation.

Chocolate. Chocolate contains a substance called theobromine that's poisonous to cats, though even more toxic to dogs. Especially if you have a multispecies home, make sure to put it in a safe place.

Houseplants. Before introducing any plant into your home, check the list of safe plants available through the ASPCA Animal Poison Control Center. Then, make the plants hard to get to with aluminum foil, decorative rocks, a vibration-sensitive alarm, or a static-charged mat. You may also try making the plants taste nasty with a little infusion of Tabasco sauce or Bitter Apple. Or, provide an alternative that your cat can chew on, such as wheatgrass or catnip.

Electrical cords. When a cat bites through an electrical cord, he can suffer electrical burns, or even a fatal shock. Make the cords as inaccessible as possible with cord guides, tape, or PVC pipe, and spray any exposed cords with Bitter Apple.

Pennies. Pennies made after 1982 are made of copper plating around a core of potentially toxic zinc. If a cat swallows this type of penny, he may suffer from red blood cell damage and even kidney damage.

Yarn, String, Rubber Bands, Thread, Tinsel. Cats are particularly fond of unraveling sweaters and ingesting the result, along with string, rubber bands, and thread. Because of the structure of a cat's tongue, it's difficult to spit such things out. The result can be internal blockage or intestinal injuries. (One reason cats tend to eat yarn is a lack of fiber in the diet; consider feeding your yarn-loving cat a small amount of canned pumpkin to compensate.)

Antifreeze. Sweet-tasting to cats—and very deadly. Each year, 120,000 pets are poisoned by antifreeze, and 90,000 of them die. Less than a teaspoon can kill a cat—just about the amount he'd find stuck to the bottom of his paws after walking through a spill. If you must change your own antifreeze, consider switching to a less toxic brand, made from propylene glycol.

If You Have an Emergency

Despite your best efforts, it is possible that your cat will eat something harmful to him. And if that happens, you need to be ready to deal with it. Keep on hand your vet's emergency number and the phone number for the ASPCA Animal Poison Control Center (888-426-4435). The center is a phone service available 24 hours a day. For a $50 consultation fee, one of the center's experienced toxicologists will advise you on what to do next with your cat. And be sure to maintain a working poison safety kit, which should include, according to the ASPCA:

fresh bottle of 3% hydrogen peroxide

can of soft cat food, as appropriate

turkey baster, bulb syringe or large medical syringe

saline eye solution to flush out eye contaminants

artificial tear gel to lubricate eyes after flushing

mild grease-cutting dishwashing liquid for the animal after skin contamination

rubber gloves

forceps to remove stingers

muzzle

pet carrier

Flea and Tick Products for Dogs. If you are tempted to use your dog's flea or tick product on your cat after an infestation or a bad tick bite, stop. If the product contains permethrin, it could be lethal to the cat.

Rodenticide (Mouse and Rat Bait). If your cat eats a dead mouse, observe him carefully. A dead rodent may have been killed by a rodenticide that could also harm your cat. Seizures, bleeding, or even death are possible results.

SUMMARY

- To thrive, all cats require animal protein in their diets. There is no such thing as completely vegetarian cat.
- The primary building blocks of complete cat foods include protein, fat, carbohydrates, vitamins, and minerals. To make sure that your cat is getting a balanced diet, it's most sensible to select from commercial brands that have met AAFCO (Association of American Feed Control Officials) trials.
- Cat food comes in three different forms: dry, semimoist, and canned. Many cat food companies also offer "lite" or "reduced calorie" versions with similar nutritional values.
- Most healthy cats do NOT need a specialized cat food formula, but cats suffering from some illnesses such as diabetes or kidney disease may prosper with a specialized diet.
- In the event that your cat eats something poisonous or harmful, make sure to have an emergency kit and the ASPCA Animal Poison Control Center's number handy (888-426-4435).

Change How and When You Feed Your Cat

Now that you've learned what to feed your cat, it's time to design a feeding schedule that slims your cat down while keeping your sanity intact.

THE VET WHO PUT 60 CATS ON A DIET

Dr. Emily Levine was looking for a few fat cats to put on a restricted calorie diet—60, to be exact. Dr. Levine, currently teaching at Lincoln University in England, conducted her study at Cornell University in 2004 over the course of 10 weeks.

What she got were hundreds of applicants clamoring to be part of the study. Because the request for research subjects ended up getting national coverage, the study received hundreds of calls from concerned owners of fat cats from all over the country. Unfortunately for the fat cats of the nation, Dr. Levine and her team were only able to accept 60 cats living in the Cornell area.

The cats who qualified for the study had to be a certain percentage over their ideal weight, which was based in part on the cat's weight at one year (if that weight had been recorded). Researchers involved in the study also based the cat's ideal weight on measurements of the cat's frame.

The requirements for the cat applicants study were simple; they had to be healthy adult overweight cats that lived exclusively indoors. (Outdoor cats simply have too many uncontrollable opportunities to feed, ranging from mice in the fields to friendly neighbors.)

The tools were also simple: one of three cat foods, a measuring cup, and a regular feeding schedule for the fat cat. None of it would have worked without dedicated owners. Dr. Levine admits that she often asked owners to sit down before showing them just what a healthy amount of cat food looked like via a measuring cup. Once they got over the shock of just how much they were overfeeding their cats, they adjusted to the new smaller portions—and the idea that they weren't really going to starve their cats.

Before they entered the study, all the cats received a thorough exam to make sure their weight wasn't being caused by other health factors. Their owners had to guarantee that for the length of the study that they could control the cat's feeding environment so that he was being fed only what the study provided—no extras from other sources.

The study's primary goal was to examine the relative weight loss effectiveness of three types of cat food—a standard maintenance for-mula food, a high fiber diet food, and a high protein diet food. The cats were divided into three groups, and their owners were instructed to feed them the required amount and no more over the course of the eight-week diet. And the results were terrific. Cats in each of the three groups lost weight. If the cat owner kept to the regimen, the cat tended to lose weight, regardless of which food group the cat was part of. Cats on the high-fiber diet food seemed to have the speediest progress, but as long as owners counted calories, the difference among the three groups wasn't significant.

Dr. Levine reports that when it comes to weight loss in cats, the fundamental things apply: A healthy fat cat will tend to lose weight if you limit his calories and increase his activity. Owners of fat cats feed their cats too much because they've lost track of what a healthy amount of food actually looks like.

If you decide to put your cat on a diet regimen, "you're going to have to hang in," Dr. Levine counsels. Nobody likes being put on a diet, especially a cat. Owners of cats in the study had to endure much pleading, yowling, and pitiful meowing. Some cats would actually lead their owners to their bowls. Give in after "the 50th meow," as Dr. Levine calls it, and you're actually giving the cat incentive to keep pleading, putting the cat on a reward schedule.

While there were a lot of success stories to come out of the study, Dr. Levine felt most proud of the cat that came into the study hefting 30 pounds. The cat's weight had contributed to a host of other health issues. The sluggish, grumpy cat wheezed when he walked, and he didn't walk very much. After a month on the diet, the cat had a "complete personality change." Freed of some of his excess pounds, the cat became a leaping, jumping, cheerful feline—and his owner was just as pleased.

KEYS TO WEIGHT LOSS

Based on her research and her veterinary practice, Dr. Levine makes the following recommendations for cat owners who are ready to get serious about their cats' weight loss:

- Have certain times that are meal times.
- Feed your cat less, but more frequently, particularly in the beginning of the diet. If you are out of the house all day, consider enlisting a family member, friend, or even a pet sitter to provide your cat with the second or third feeding of the day during the first couple weeks of the diet. If that isn't possible, feed your cat once in the morning, a second time as soon as you get home, and a third time as an evening snack.
- Restrict meals to one place.
- Measure your cat's food.
- Use snacks wisely and sparingly.
- Make the food entertaining—consider putting some of the cat's dry food in a Buster Cube toy, which releases the food slowly as the cat plays with the toy.
- Weigh your cat religiously every two weeks on a scale that measures by the ounce, as well as by the pound; it's the only way to accurately establish your cat's weight loss. You can purchase a pet scale through a large pet supply company for around $50, or you might investigate a baby scale. Otherwise, make a standing appointment to visit your vet every two weeks to weigh your cat. Dr. Levine emphasizes that an accurate record is a vital tool in a cat's weight loss program.
- Aim for slow, gradual weight loss; putting your fat cat on a crash

diet puts him at risk for hepatic lipidosis, an often-fatal liver disease. If your dieting cat exhibits lethargy or unusual vomiting, take him to the vet immediately.

- Expect resistance; assume that your cat will not welcome the change, and be strong.
- Consider starting with a high fiber food that makes your cat feel full.

CAT FOOD TYPES
What Is Dry Food, And Why Should I Feed It To My Cat?

It's fast, it's easy, and you can leave it out all day. It's dry kibble. There are lots of advantages for humans—it's simple to measure and you can leave it in the bowl all day without danger of spoiling.

But in a fat cat household, kibble abuse is common. Leave a bowl out for a bored fat cat, and the cat gorges himself without stopping.

Additionally, you lose an opportunity for a training moment with your cat if you just dump the kibble out in the bowl and walk away. At one three-cat home, the human owner insists that each cat "work" for

One Fat Minute

While cats don't form packs the way dogs do, they are still social creatures, and they want to bond with you, and, unlike dogs, they rarely have an organized activity to bond around. So, often, mealtime can be the only time you bond with your cat. Think about hand-feeding your cat at least one meal a day. Not only will this help you get an accurate sense of how much you should be feeding your cat—it increases the bond between you and your cat.

Nerp, a disabled kitty, gets extra bonding from his owner with spoonfed meals.

his or her bowl before getting fed by doing a trick. And some people like to split the kibble up—one part for feeding, one part for training. If you must be away from your dieting cat for days at a time, you might want to invest in an automated feeder that releases a certain amount of food on a schedule.

What Is Wet Food, And Why Should I Feed It To My Cat?

If your cat could speak as you open her canned food, she would tell you how tasty she finds it. How she might want to eat more and more and more. If you didn't know better.

In addition to convenience, canned food is a good choice for cats who are older, or who are recovering from an illness. Cats with diabetes or those suffering from urinary tract problems also appear to do better on a canned diet, possibly because of the canned food's high water content. Older cats may find canned food easier to digest.

But canned food has a couple of disadvantages. It's expensive. The temptation not to measure an exact amount of food is strong when you just "open a can." Also, canned food remains fresh for only a couple of days…in human time. Many cats turn their highly tuned noses up long before the canned food doesn't smell good to you. However, there are ways around a cat's disdain for already opened canned food. When presenting your cat with open canned food, try microwaving it for a few seconds to bring it up to cat satisfaction. Warm food can convince a finicky cat.

Semimoist Food

Other choices include semimoist foods, usually in interesting shapes and colors, which are more visually appealing to humans, but your cat's mileage may vary. Focus on calories and taste, and always keep track of how much you're feeding your cat.

WATER BOWL ETIQUETTE

As we discussed in the previous chapter, water is just as important to humans as to cats. Although your cat does not need to drink the same eight glasses you do, you'll want to make sure you encourage them to drink what they need; on average, this is about 8 to 10 ounces of water per day. Keep in mind that cats who exclusively eat canned food, which is dense with water, may need less, and cats who exclusively eat dry kibble may need a little more.

Your cat's water bowl should be thoroughly cleaned at least once a day. Refresh the water often. Your cat's nose will detect water that's "off" long before you will.

If your cat is a finicky water drinker, consider buying a refreshing fountain from a pet supply store. Cats will not tell you when they are dehydrated, and they dehydrate very easily. It's important not to skimp on something this vital.

Unless you really can't handle it, don't discourage your cat from drinking from the faucet; he is just following a natural instinct to go after a very fresh water supply. On the other hand, do discourage your cat from seeking water in the toilet bowl. Between the likelihood of detergents and bacteria, it's not something you really want your cat consuming. Not to mention that he could fall in. For all kinds of reasons, if you have a cat, keep your toilet lid down.

As your cat ages, keep track of his water intake. A suddenly increase in water consumption could mean the onset of diabetes or kidney problems.

If your cat does refuse regular tap water, consider filtered or even designer "distilled" water. Distilling removes normal minerals from water, and therefore may benefit cats with urinary tract problems who are prone to forming crystals in their urine.

SO, WHAT DOES A CAT DIET LOOK LIKE?

Though it is important both physically and psychologically to get your fat cat to move more, your primary tool in your cat's weight loss plan is fewer calories. What follows are a few sample diet plans, using examples of current dry, semi-moist, and canned foods on the market, for a variety of sizes of adult cats. Depending on your cat's activity and metabolic levels, you may have to adjust upwards or downwards on the suggested quantities. This is why, if you're serious about weight loss for your cat, it's important to establish exactly how much your fat cat weighs at the beginning of the diet, and, subsequently, to weigh him at least once every two weeks on a scale that shows pounds and ounces. And it's equally vital to accurately count the calories of all the food you're giving your cat, from table scraps to gourmet kitty cuisine.

Sample Fat Cat Weight Loss Diet 1

Cat weight: 8 pounds

Food type: dry lamb meat and rice weight control formula, approximately 350 calories per 8 ounce cup

Feeding instructions: serve 1/2 cup total daily of a dry weight control formula; when goal is achieved, increase quantity to 3/4 cup

Frequency: If your cat is used to being fed all the time, ease the transition by feeding him four times a day, if possible, 1/8 cup of food per session. If your cat is more flexible, feed 3 times a day, 1/6 of a cup a session. Ideally, you'll be able to cut back to 2 feedings a day, 1/4 cup each session.

Sample Fat Cat Weight Loss Diet 2

Cat weight: 12 pounds

Food type: semimoist weight control tuna pouches, approximately 68 calories per 3 ounce pouch

Feeding instructions: serve daily a total of 3-1/2 pouches; when goal is achieved, increase to approximately 4 to 5-1/2 pouches

Frequency: If your cat is used to being fed all the time, ease the transition by feeding him four times a day, if possible, 1 pouch for each of 3 sessions, and 1/2 pouch for the final feeding. If you're feeding 3 times a day, try 1 pouch + 1 pouch + 1-1/2 pouches. Ideally, you'll be able to cut back to 2 feedings a day, 2 pouches for the big meal, 1-1/2 pouches for the smaller meal.

Sample Fat Cat Weight Loss Diet 3

Cat weight: 4 pounds

Food type: canned chicken and rice weight control formula, 6 ounce portion, approximately 205 calories

Feeding instructions: serve daily a total of 1/3 of a can; when goal is achieved, increase to 1/2 to 2/3 of a can

Frequency: While this may look like a small amount of food, it is possible to divide it into three portions. Particularly if your cat is used to having a large amount of food around all day, you might want to use each of the three sessions (and the food) to do a little obedience training—asking your cat to come when called, for instance, and then providing the serving. This will help you keep track of how much your cat is eating, and it will help you bond with your cat. Later on, you may want to reduce the feedings to 1/6 of a can, twice a day.

These cases suggest what a diet looks like when you stick strictly to one of the three general types of cat food. Can you—should you—mix different types of foods, spicing up your kitty's kibble with semi-moist morsels? Absolutely, if it helps make your cat more comfortable with the diet. Remember, however, to calculate the calories of all the food you give your cat, regardless of type. Check the food package, or check the food company's Web site. If you can't locate it, call the company's customer support line. They will be happy to help you establish an accurate calorie count, and even estimate the portion to slim down your cat.

SUMMARY

- When it comes to putting your cat on a diet, research suggests that the two most important factors are finding a food your cat enjoys and limiting the number of calories he eats.
- Many cats go through a difficult period of begging and nagging when first put on a diet. It's up to the owners to hang in until the cat adjusts.
- Cat food comes in three formats—dry, semimoist, and canned. Dry food keeps better than canned food, while canned food can be both expensive—and a lifesaver for finicky cats. Semimoist food is sometimes used to "spice up" less tasty dry food.
- Make sure to track your cat's water intake, as well as his food.

6

Exercise Your Cat at Home

One of the first things you'll notice in the Animal Planet show "Pet Star," the pet version of "American Idol," is the scarcity of cats. Dogs will do anything, parrots plead for the judges' love, and horses will count to ten for a $2,500 prize—or just the audience's applause.

But not most cats. Cats have better things to do, it seems, than raise flags, dance a Scottish jig, or do simple math. They'd rather be sleeping up to 16 hours a day.

But is it completely true? Or is it something that you've come to believe?

Unlike dogs, cats were not bred for a lot of jobs, nor, until very recently, were they trained to play in structured ways the way dogs and other larger mammals do. They were not trained to endure, lift, haul, or rescue. So unlike dogs, cats don't actually benefit by long, aerobically-taxing bouts of play. They sprint, dart, prowl and hide, mimicking their ancestors hunting in the wild. The most successful forms of play for cats evoke some of their ancient primeval spirit.

If your cat is slightly or significantly overweight, overeating is clearly part of the equation. But lack of activity is the other. And while cats can and do find ways to amuse themselves, from toilet paper rolls to balled-up tissues, they generally move more when they move with you.

Fat Cat Quiz

1. What kind of exercise does your cat typically get?
2. Do you know what cat play looks like?
3. Does your cat enjoy playing with people? Other cats? Or (gasp) other kinds of pets in the household? Is your cat a day feline or a night feline?
4. How many toys does your cat have? What kind?
5. Do you regularly refresh (that is, hide) your cat's toys?

Answers

1. While even the largest cat doesn't need hours of exercise to stay fit, every cat benefits from moving around, whether it's following you from room to room (try leading him with a treat), or playing a fast game of "chase the toy." If your cat has become a feline couch potato, you know to start slow. But you could start today with two 30-second play sessions.
2. Cat play has a start and stop quality that doesn't look (to the average dog owner) like playing at all. It is much more modeled on the hunt that cat's ancestors performed in the wild. When play-

ing with your cat and using a cat toy, try to think and move like a mouse who's fleeing for his life. Your cat will really enjoy it.

3. Cats, like people, have all different kinds of socializing skills. Some cats are solitary hunters. Other cats love to wrestle with their pals. Still others (fewer others) enjoy hanging out with and playing with the dog. And, of course, lots of cats relish time with you. One of the ways to increase your fat cat's activity is to spend a few days really noticing just when your cat plays the most—and plays the most happily. You may find that your supposedly sluggish cat becomes a dynamo at night, when your significant other comes home. Or that your pokey pussycat really loves chasing dogs.

4. It may sound like a silly question, but the fact is, there are some very well-fed, well-loved cats whose owners don't think toys are important. All mammals learn and grow through play. Play is a powerful weapon against your cat's boredom, and while it's not necessary to buy a toy for every day in the month, having a few toys on hand to get your cat excited also stimulates your creativity.

5. This is an outgrowth of the previous question. At zoos, they call it "environmental enrichment." Translated into plain English, that means giving cats something to look forward to, keeping them a little bit on edge. If you have young children, you may already be familiar with the idea of putting away some of their toys for a few weeks, and then bringing them out—surprise!—as if they were new. This toy rotation works equally well with cats. It also keeps the owners fresh. As human beings, we can get into some very deep ruts. We don't have to make our cats follow us into the ruts.

HOW MUCH IS ENOUGH?

If your cat could, he would probably want to play with you all day…between naps. But if you are starting an exercise program with a genuinely fat cat, start small and slow. Even 30 seconds of playing will rev up your cat's metabolism. Shoot for short, but frequent, exercise breaks a couple of times a day until they become a habit. In the beginning, keep track of this the way you track your cat's food.

If you're convinced that you already play with your cats plenty, but are seeing no weight loss, you may want to take your cat to the next level with cat clicker training, or even cat agility.

CAT AGILITY

Cats lazy? The creators of cat agility don't seem to think so. Of course your cat is agile, but compete in a structured game? Cat agility as a competitive event began in 2003, taking as its inspiration dog agility events—which were originally inspired by horse agility events. Cat agility events are generally open to all kinds of cats, regardless of breed. All your cat has to be is all-cat, according to co-founder Vickie Shields, and show up.

Currently, you'll find most cat agility events at cat shows, where the current cat agility practitioners are often showing their cats in official competition.

What does the cat agility course look like?

"Cats are more '3-D' than dogs," explains Shields, who describes the course as a flexible 30 x 30 foot area that easily adapts to a cat's age and skill abilities. The equipment is strong, but easily portable.

What does competitive cat agility involve?

First and foremost, it involves giving the cat time to relax. Then, the cat is led by its owner through a series of physical challenges from jumping through hoops to standing on platforms, all designed to show off the cat's natural agility and physical daring—and make the owner connect with her cat.

While Shields says that no particular breed has shown more agility prowess than any other, she does think that at the current time, the males have the edge. The age of the cat doesn't seem to matter, or the breed, or the size. Just the spirit.

If you are interested in formal cat agility, you can log on to their Web site for an upcoming calendar (www.catagility.com) and more resources, including instructional videos. If you'd like to start practicing in your home, all you really need are a couple of chairs, an embroidery hoop, some treats, and some patience. For examples of a homegrown agility course, check out www.friskies.com, which offers quick tips for making your cat more agile—whether it's jumping through an embroidery hoop, or racing through a 30 x 30 agility course seven times.

CLICKER TRAINING

Have you ever dreamed of having your cat retrieve? Clicker training may help you fulfill your dream. Clicker training, originally used with large animals such as dolphins and horses, hit the mainstream of dog training about the same time the Internet became popular. While the population of owners and trainers clicker training their cats is much smaller, clicker trainer enthusiasts insist that cats, despite their independent nature, can also be trained via clicker training.

Sue Gilsdorf, a trauma nurse by profession, is a passionate cat clicker trainer. Currently the owner of three male cats, Sue originally got involved in clicker training when she found herself at her wit's end with a new adult male cat she'd adopted, Big Bad Ratuie, who displayed severe behavioral problems, including beating up on Sue's original cat Acacia, an old female. Guided by an animal behaviorist, Sue not only extinguished Big Bad Ratuie's big bad behaviors, but taught him to wait by his food bowl, retrieve, and kiss noses. This so inspired Sue, she put her other cats on a clicker regimen—and actually trained her old female cat, Acacia, to eat on schedule, slim down, and work for treats. Now her younger cat Tazz is learning how to walk on a ball. All of her cats are slim and healthy, and, thanks to the clicker training, highly bonded to her.

Getting Started

To use clicker training, obviously, you need a clicker, which you can purchase from a toy store, a pet supply store, or a clicker training Web site. Then you need treats—and a plan.

Before you begin working with your cat, sit down and think about what exactly it is you would like the cat to do.

Repeat: think about what it is that you would like the cat to DO.

If you immediately begin thinking of what you DON'T want the cat to do, make that list up, too. (Once you get comfortable with clicker training, you can positively train some bad habits away.)

Once you begin:

- Break the desired behavior into the smallest possible steps
- Train your cat just before a meal, but don't starve your cat
- When the cat delivers the behavior, click and immediately treat
- Hold the reward treat in a spoon; it makes it easier to move your cat from place to place
- Focus on one trick at a time, and do it in a quiet environment
- Keep the training sessions short, 10-15 minutes

For further instruction, try Karen Pryor's *Clicker Training for Cats*, or sign up at Wendy Jeffries' cat clicker Yahoo group at **groups. yahoo.com/group/Cat-Clicker/**.

Some cats, like Ratuie, enjoy clicker training.

ENVIRONMENTAL ENRICHMENT

Getting your exclusively indoor cat more active involves enriching your cat's environment. That's less complicated than it sounds. Translated, it breaks down into two big categories: supplying your cat with toys, and providing cat-friendly furniture.

Toys

It's no big secret, if you play with your cat for any length of time, that most cats can be satisfied with very, very simple toys, for example, a piece of string and a paper bag, and your cat's in heaven. There are lots of places on the Web (and several books) that will turn you into a mad cat toy inventor, if you choose. (Remember to put a string away after you play with the cat; your cat may decide the best thing to do with his string toy is to swallow it.)

But if you'd like to get beyond the dancing string and the tumbling paper bag, there's a gigantic world of cat toys out there for you. Keep in mind, even if you do buy toys that your cat can play with by himself, when you've got a fat cat, make sure you are scheduling regular play sessions with your cat.

One Web site (**cattoys.com**) actually organizes its toys not just by brand, but by type of cat (active to less active, solitary to social, even "night owl"). Actually figuring out what kind of cat you have may help you encourage your cat in that little extra bit of exercise, or provide the nocturnal cat with a toy that will keep him occupied while you're snoozing.

Popular toys on the market include:

Toys on a wand and string, such as Da Bird, which encourages you, the owner, to dangle and dance some kind of a lure, such as a feather, to get your cat to respond. Remember to store these toys when you're not around; you don't want your kitty getting snarled in a line.

Other toys that offer lures include a glove decorated with giant pompoms. You manipulate the glove while the cat bats the pompoms: big fun.

Cat-solo toys include furry fake mice (the appeal here is obvious), and a variety of textured toys that can be seasoned with catnip, over and over again.

The Cat Dancer, made of spring loaded wire and curled up paper, doesn't look like much to human eyes, but claims to be the "original cat interaction toy," allegedly the favorite of Calvin Klein's late cat, Max. Though the original Cat Dancer is meant for owner plus cat, the manufacturer now offers a version with a wall mount so that the toy can be used safely when the cat is alone.

Whatever toys you choose, ask yourself: who else will be using the toy? If you have other pets, such a chew-toy happy dogs, your supposedly safe little cat-friendly big foam ball could be chewed into some very unsafe small pieces. Better safe than sorry: Put all "interactive" toys away after a play session, and make careful choices for the toys that your cat plays with alone. Remember, also, that babies and small children can also get into mischief with a cat toy, so childproof accordingly.

Cat Furniture

Cats are three-dimensional creatures. They love to run, jump, and hide. Especially when you're trying to get your fat cat to move more, look for ways to make your cat's environment more inviting.

There is a wealth of cat furniture out there, from the simple scratching post to floor to ceiling towers that look like Donald Trump owns them. Some people have even redesigned their houses so that their cats can actually run from room to room via a series of portals, shelves, and steps. (See **www.thecatshouse.com** for a cat's paradise, created by two artists for their ten cats.)

Whatever you choose, consider the following:

- Make sure that the furniture has a stable base, and that any cat shelves or perches are well-mounted.
- If you're in a multi-cat family, consider buying one tower per cat.
- Scratching matters; look for materials that will encourage your cats to scratch safely.

- If your cat is older, consider investing in a set of steps up to the window where he used to jump.
- Invite access to windowsills, as long as the window stays closed. Cats love to watch the action outside!

WHEN CATS NEED REHABILITATION

If your cat is injured, that can obviously affect his ability and inclination to exercise. Make sure you talk to your doctor about ways to keep your cat moving without impeding his healing process. There are some services for cats who need rehabilitation, including physical therapy and acupuncture.

Physical Therapy

Twenty years ago, recommending physical therapy for a pet would have been a joke, but it is now joining the mainstream. For many years massage and strengthening exercises have been required after a human recovers from surgery. Why not a cat? Currently, pet physical therapy may include therapeutic exercise, manual exercise, therapeutic massage, ultrasound, heat, cold, and other techniques.

When looking for reputable physical therapy, begin with referrals from your vet, or nearest animal hospital, or check the Web site of the American Veterinary Medical Association (**www.avma.org/care-foranimals/default.asp**) regarding complementary and alternative medicine. Physical therapy for pets is still a very new field; don't jeopardize your pet's health. Ideally, you are looking for someone who is both licensed in physical therapy and experienced with pets.

Acupuncture

You may think that your cat might not be crazy about acupuncture, and you might be right. But research is growing, both in the human and pet communities, that proves it is an effective treatment for a variety of conditions, from arthritis to anxiety, and the results are promising. During acupuncture, specific points on the body are stimulated to bring about changes in the musculo-skeletal, nervous, endocrine, cardiovascular, and immune systems. Stimulation may be done with needles, injections, electrodes, or even lasers.

Dr. Martha Gearhart, D.V.M., of Pleasant Valley Animal Hospital, is certified by the International Veterinary Acupuncture Society. She used acupuncture to treat Erica, a tough 18-year-old tortoiseshell cat suffering from slow kidney failure, an inflexible spine, and walking problems. Dr. Gearhart administered acupuncture to alleviate Erica's pain and keep her moving, and it's been a success. Thanks to acupuncture, Erica remains a mobile, happy cat.

SUMMARY

- Cats need to be encouraged to move—but once they are, they won't stop.
- Agility training is becoming more commonplace with cats.
- Clicker training is an effective way to get your cat more active, and more fit.
- Choose toys that match your cat's personality and your life style.
- Buy or build shelves and towers that will give cats more opportunity to move and run.
- "Human" therapies such as acupuncture and physical therapy are becoming more common in feline medicine.

Explore the Great Outdoors with Your Cat

In the old days, cats went everywhere in the outside world—but didn't live that long. Unlike contemporary dogs, present-day cats rarely spend much time outside. This chapter covers how to introduce your kitty to the outside world, and when; as well as medical and physical precautions to take before taking your cat into the wild world, from vaccinations to harnesses.

Until the middle of the 20th century, even the best-loved cat faced a series of cruel threats in the outside world, and usually, the result was pretty grim. Then, the inventor of kitty litter, Edward Lowe, and his invention, radically changed the life of all cats. The result, less than sixty years later, has been an exponential growth in cats as house pets, so much so that the average cat-owning household now has more than one.

Many cat lovers feel it is unfair to take a cat outside, given the dangers (although this is an attitude much more prevalent in the U.S. than in Great Britain, where many more cats are raised indoor/outdoor).The lifespan of an outdoor cat is significantly shorter (according to the ASPCA Web site, an indoor cat will outlive an outdoor cat by an average of eight years).

Still, there are a few good reasons for your cat to learn how to go outside, and it is important to note that not all threats to cats are outside. Many cats can get themselves into plenty of trouble without ever venturing outside. Some cats, because of health issues, can't use a litter box and need to go outside to do their business. And it's clear that some cats are just happier outside. Remember, however, that unlike dogs, cats have NOT been bred to work the fields, herd sheep, hunt down rats, or provide search and rescue. Cats see the outdoors as territory and hunting ground, pretty much. Putting your cat outside expands his sense of territory, for good and for not so good. Outdoor cats are typically adventurous—but also less connected to their inside home base than indoor cats, and therefore, to you. They have heard the call of the wild, and that means they may listen less to the call of you.

THE CAT'S BACKYARD

Probably the best way to have your cat experience the outside world is to let him experience it in an enclosed porch. But what if you don't have a porch? What if all you have is a backyard?

The first rule to letting your cat play outside in your backyard is this: Get a cat-secure fence.

That means secure FOR your cat, and secure AGAINST anything that might want to attack your cat. In order to that, it's important to do two things.

1. Think like a cat.
2. And then: think like something or someone who might want to hurt your cat.

You may think of your cat as a mighty hunter, but other predatory animals, particularly in rural environments, will see your cat as a tasty treat.

You may let your cat loll around in a fenced-in yard, but make sure that the bottom edge of the fence doesn't allow for your nimble cat (or something else) to slither beneath it. The top part of the fence looks like the top of a maximum security prison to you—but does it look that way to your cat?

And how well does the fenced-in area protect your cat against the elements—not just rain or snow, but any winds that might blow something sharp into your cat's turf?

If you decide against a permanent fence, take heart. Pet supply companies such as Drs. Foster and Smith (www.drsfostersmith.com) now offer collapsible metal-and-mesh enclosures that allow you to give your cat a taste of the outdoors, while requiring no major yard renovation.

BEYOND THE BACKYARD: GOING FOR A WALK

Before making the decision to move your cat farther into the outside world, make sure you can get your cat back. And the way to do that is simple: give your cat a collar, an ID, a harness, a leash, and, ideally, a

Not all cats are as limber, or spend as much time oudoors, as Jinx.

tattoo or a microchip. Invest in a figure 8 harness, not a collar, and make sure that it fits comfortably. You can't use a dog's collar; it's too heavy. Ask your vet to microchip your cat, and be sure to register the number on the chip with AKC Companion Animal Recovery (800-252-7894), which, for a $12.50 fee, offers a lifetime, 24-hour, year-round identification service for dogs, cats, horses, lizards, rabbits, birds, and any other companion animal wearing a chip. They also offer a tag with the cat's ID number and the recovery center's number, which could be very helpful if the person who locates your cat doesn't have a microchip scanner handy.

Make sure that your cat's vaccinations are up to date. If they aren't, vaccinate first, take your cat outside second.

If you've never walked a cat, be prepared for an amble. Cats will mosey in a way that makes a beagle's pokey sniffing seem like a marathon run. Cats don't have the genetic history of leisurely strolls with a master, or purposeful hunts with a mistress. Cats are used to seeing the outside as territory to be assessed, selected, and explored.

When first exposing your cat to the outside world, keep it brief and as low stress as possible. Choose an off-time of the day, where your cat is likely to encounter as few threats and distractions as possible. Many dogs will not be glad to see a cat walking around, and will make their best efforts to announce that. (There are exceptions to the rule. In the town where this writer lives, she used to see a cat walked by his owner. Not only did the cat wear a harness quite happily, it also wore…a sweater. Some dogs wouldn't threaten the cat at all…just halt in amazement at the strange sight.)

How do you expose your cat to the great outdoors *without* having him either find snacks on his own, or get fed by friends? The answer seems to boil down to three words: Control his environment. If you walk your cat on a leash, it is quite possible that somebody will want to give your adorable cat a treat of some kind. Explain to the treat-giver that your cat's on a special diet, and can only eat certain things—because that's the truth.

If you're letting your cat wander in your backyard for exercise, make sure that it is very well fenced, so your cat can't escape, and, if at all possible, make sure that your backyard hasn't become a haven for mice. If it has, either keep your cat's outdoor visits to a few well-supervised minutes, or, if your cat's determined to go after the mice, adjust his diet accordingly.

Finally, don't let your cat roam unleashed through the neighborhood, whether it's a concrete city block or a country road. Your cat may return to you, having feasted at your neighbors' places for second and third breakfast. Or he may not return at all. If he doesn't return to you, it may be because somebody decided your cat would make a good target—or even a good meal.

OUTSIDE ISN'T FOR EVERYONE

Please understand: If your cat does not enjoy going outside, respect his wishes. If you have a multi-cat family, it's probably best that all cats stay indoor cats. It also should go without saying that no declawed cat should ever go outside. A declawed cat lacks the tools to defend himself. This goes double for cats with disabilities such as deafness or lameness; they are just too vulnerable. Give them a good life inside.

When your cat goes out, he interacts with the natural world. This means trees and flowers and sunshine…and fleas and vermin and predators, including dogs. Even fellow cats can cause trouble to your outdoor cat. A "normal" bite from another healthy cat still means your cat runs the risk of an abscess, thanks to the bacteria that dwells in every healthy cat. If you suspect your cat has an abscess, drain it immediately and sterilize the area, or take your cat to the vet.

That's just the beginning of the dangers. A bite from a sick cat exposes your cat to the possibility of feline leukemia, feline immunodeficiency virus, or feline infectious peritonitis. All are big risks for the small pleasure of knowing your cat is roaming the neighborhood.

Know that by taking your cat outside, you are probably in a minority. In a poll published in the January 2005 Cat Fancy, 10 percent of the readers responding to a poll said that their cat had developed an abscess from an outdoor cat fight. The relatively good news is that 15 percent of the readers said that their cats went outside and remained free from abscesses. But the vast majority of the readers who responded—a full 75 percent—agreed with the statement: "No, I minimize risks by always keeping my cat inside."

SUMMARY

- If you take the right precautions, it is possible to take your cat outside.
- Cats should be microchipped or tattooed, vaccinated, and on a harness leash when walking outside.
- When "catproofing" your backyard, remember that you are both trying to keep your cat inside and all threats to him outside.
- Temporary outdoor environments offer a way for your cat to enjoy the outside without renovating your backyard.

Help Your Older Cat Adjust

Thanks to advances in veterinary science and the enormous increase in the number of exclusively indoor cats, many cats are living into their late teens and early twenties. Healthy longevity is becoming the rule, not the exception. So how do you keep your old cat as trim and as fit as possible?

Old age reaches each cat at a different time, but most vets would consider any cat over the age of 10 as an "older cat." When a cat is 12, he is about the equivalent of human 65, and at 20, has reached his 100th birthday. The signs of aging creep up slowly on a healthy old cat, but they may include:

Decline of the senses. This includes vision, hearing, and smell. If your cat seems less interested in eating, remember that heat intensifies smell. Warm canned cat food in the microwave, and see if your cat doesn't perk up.

Loss of muscle mass. Your cat may seem smaller, more bony, less physically agile.

Drier, or less tidy coat. You may have to help your cat groom as he ages.

Increased sleeping. This may indicate illness, or could be typical slowing down.

AGE-RELATED ILLNESSES

While cats can suffer from the following illnesses at nearly any age, they seem to occur more often among elderly cats:

Diabetes. If your fat cat rapidly loses a lot of weight while eating in large quantities, and can't satisfy his thirst, there is strong chance that he is diabetic. Usual treatment includes changes in diet and medication, possibly insulin injection. Take your cat to the vet immediately if he shows these signs and get your cat tested.

Hyperthyroidism. If your fat cat is eating like there's no tomorrow, and yet losing weight, it's possible that he suffers from an overactive thyroid. The treatment of choice these days is radioactive iodine therapy, which takes 7 to 14 days in isolation to complete, because your cat is radioactive and must be kept away from other people. The good news is, the therapy is 90-95% effective. Surgery and medication are also options.

Obstipation. Obstipation is the complete inability to defecate. If you suspect your cat of having obstipation, monitor his litter box activity. Obstipation can be resolved, in some cases, by drugs, laxatives, attention to your cat's grooming (obstipation is sometimes caused by a cat's excessive intake of his own hair), or surgery.

Tullie, an overweight elder cat, has just begun his diet.

IF YOUR CAT IS HEALTHY...

And you want to keep him there, consider the following:

- Keep him warm and well-supported. Dogs are more prone to prefer orthopedic beds, but you might want to plunk down a few orthopedic mats, just to give your cat a soft landing.
- If he's begun to shrug off his food, consider microwaving any kind of food, just so that it feels hot.

- Brush his teeth, if you haven't started already. Now is the time to make sure that your cat retains all of his teeth and fight off periodontal disease, which is also implicated in infections in other parts of the body.
- Take him for regular check-ups, which include dental cleaning, blood, and urine tests.

REDUCING YOUR OLDER FAT CAT

The weight loss regimen for an older cat remains the same. Move more, eat less. Your aging cat's metabolism doesn't slow down as much as an aging dog's, but it is likely that arthritis and other age-related ailments may make your older cat a little less mobile.

Keep him exercised. Do less, but more often. If he's begun to shun his more high-flying toys and furniture, look for stuff that's a little easier to climb.

Keep him trim, but don't push it. Elder cats shouldn't lose more than 1.5 percent of their body weight per week (as opposed to 2 percent for younger cats). You'll probably be feeding your cat less food, but more often. If your cat suddenly stops eating, take him to the vet immediately.

SENIOR CAT FOOD

Do senior cats need special "senior" food?

Some studies indicate that older cats (defined as cats in the last third of their lives) don't digest fat as well as younger cats, so feeding your older cat a senior food that contains a more digestible fat is a good idea. Older cats also do not absorb vitamins and minerals as well as younger cats, so look for a formula that includes additional vitamins (particularly B vitamins and balanced minerals).

Beyond that, should you add vitamin supplements to your older cat's chow? According to an article by Karen Lee Stevens in the February 2005 issue of CatWatch, released through the Cornell University Feline Health Center, probably not, if the cat is being fed a standard commercial diet. Well-meaning owners who give their older cats high doses of vitamin D to prevent brittle bones, for example, may actually induce skeletal abnormalities.

If your cat suffers from dental problems, or seems to have trouble eating hard kibble, you may want to look into food that is smaller and/or easier to chew. For instance, switching from dry to a mixture of dry and wet, or switching over to wet food entirely. As with any diet transition, make the switch gradually, over several days.

With some senior cats, the issue isn't food, but water. Some older cats tend to drink less water than they should, which may exacerbate constipation or kidney problems. Hydration is the key here; the higher water content of canned foods may be a good choice—or perhaps just improving your cat's water source. Because of a cat's highly developed sense of smell, perfectly good water in a bowl may smell "off" to him. Encourage your cat to drink more water—even consider purchasing a running water fountain for your kitty.

SUPPLEMENTS FOR YOUR OLDER CAT'S JOINTS

If your vet has given your older cat a clean bill of health, you may want to give him a supplement containing glucosamine and chondroitin, which appears to help humans, dogs, and cats with arthritis and joint problems. Be aware, however, that because supplements, unlike drugs, aren't regulated, the quality and quantity of supplements vary greatly. Try to research supplements before purchasing them.

WHEN YOUR CAT HAS SPECIAL CHALLENGES

Like humans, cats may become more prone to accidents and illnesses as they become older, and this can lead to various disabilities. And of course, like humans, some cats are born disabled. Whether your cat's problem is temporary or permanent, stay calm. You may view your cat as having lost something, whether it's hearing, sight, mobility, balance, or even some combination of conditions, but your cat may be able to adjust without sacrificing any quality of life. As far as exercise goes, a three-legged cat may have to slow down a little jumping from place to place, but she can still jump—and she will. A blind or deaf cat may not have the run of your backyard—but she could rule your roost at home. A cat with cerebellar hypoplasia may not move like a lot of cats…but she will move. Dealing with a cat with a disability may mean redefining your image of "fit cat." It will definitely change your life.

The chief permanent disabilities that afflict cats fall into the following categories:

Blindness. Many cats suffer from sight impairment, ranging from mild to total. Their senses of smell and hearing are often heightened—so much so that sometimes their owners don't realize that they're blind for quite a bit of time. To keep your blind cat active, routine is vital. A blind cat often uses scent and memory to keep track of where he is, and where he's going. Alternately, a sightless cat sometimes gently "bumps" into objects to get his bearings.

Deafness. Some cats are born deaf. Others lose their hearing through illness or aging. Helping your deaf cat to thrive physically depends on developing a consistent set of physical signals—usually visual, sometimes tactile—to replace the spoken commands given to a hearing cat. As far as keeping your deaf kitty fit, there are really no limits—as long as you keep your cat inside. When it comes to going outside, deaf cats lack all of a hearing cat's normal defenses. They can't hear a car backing up, or a dog approaching. While you may feel that you are denying your cat part of her birthright, you are actually extending her life.

Mobility Impairment. One of the most common disabilities in cats is the loss of a single leg, often through cancer or an accident, which turns the cat into a "tripod." Thanks to the miracle of a cat's weight distribution, most three-legged cats get around nearly as fast as their four-legged siblings, though cats missing a rear leg can't jump as high, and cats missing a front leg must work harder at landings. Obesity is even more dangerous for tripod cats than the general cat population. Because balance is especially critical in a tripod cat, any excess weight severely taxes the cat's surviving three legs, and puts him at risk for arthritis. And while your three-legged titan may seem to crave the outside world, it is probably best to resist the temptation. He may move around like a house afire, but he is also a cat whose internal organs are more exposed, making him vulnerable to attack.

Many cats can, and do, get along with only the front legs functional. When a cat's back legs become paralyzed, or, in some cases, amputated, more and more cat owners are turning to some form of wheelchair or cart. HandicappedPets.com offers resources and products for owners of handicapped pets, from temporary splints to slings, wheelchairs, carts, and ramps. HandicappedPets.com also offers visitors an active bulletin board where owners of handicapped pets can provide support, swap stories, resell equipment, and even donate to help a pet in need of an assistive device. Even if your pet is only temporarily disabled, this Web site can prove a gold mine of support and information.

Cerebellar Hypoplasia. Cats with cerebellar hypoplasia (CH) experience muscular spasms and tremors, and compromised coordination. Some wobble a little. Some wobble a lot. They cannot, and never will be, outdoor cats. But they can be great cats. It's important to provide CH cats with a lot of physical support; CH cats often like to orient themselves by leaning again something, such as a wall, or the side of a litter box, in order to stabilize themselves. Owner of CH cats have a number of Internet resources to help them cope, among them, the CH Kitty Club (**www.chkittyclub.com**) and the Yahoo group e-mail list, Handicats (**groups.yahoo.com/group/handicats/**).

SUMMARY

- Older cats in good health show their age in a variety of ways, from a diminishment of senses to more limited mobility.
- Older cats can lose weight, but should do it more slowly than a middle-aged or young cat would.
- With age, often comes disability ranging from blindness to paralysis. Thanks to the Web and improved medical care, these cats can lead long and healthy lives.

Deal with a
Multi-Pet Household

Do you feel that the best fitness coach for your fat cat could be another pet?

You could be right.

And you could be wrong.

Since the dawn of comics and cartoons, as pet owners, we've seen too many images of a peaceable kingdom, filled with multiple cats and dogs and other assorted members of the menagerie. And while it's good to take inspiration from fictional stories, it's important to remember that it's just that: fiction.

Still, multi-cat families are common—that's why cats have eclipsed dogs as the most popular pet in the United States.

The truth is that conflict is typical, and to be expected. One multi-pet family has split their Brooklyn apartment into three equal kingdoms: one area for the husband's cat, one for the wife's cat, and another area for the

Chihuahua mix they adopted together. We're not quite sure what would happen if they had to move to a smaller apartment. Probably the people would move out and the animals would stay.

So, make sure that you really are ready for a second pet, including the expense, the extra labor, the extra vet visits, and the potential for conflict.

Some cat combos are better than others. The worst combination in the world is an old cat with…almost anyone else. Old cats like their routine, and a new kitten or full-grown cat is a major upset in routine. Equally unpleasant are two sexually intact adult males. The territory fights will never end.

The optimal configuration is two spayed or neutered indoor cats, one slightly smaller than the other, with differing, but harmonious, personalities. It may be difficult to tell when you're adopting the second cat, but do your best to find out—two male cats who clearly think of themselves as Kings of the House is a no-no, for example. A more ideal combo would be an outgoing cat paired with a shy cat, for example. This can mean a pair of kittens, a pair of cats, or an established middle-aged cat with a young adult cat.

Once you've decided you're ready, and you've picked a cat, proceed with the preparation process.

INTRODUCING THE NEW CAT

Before you bring the new cat home, make sure that you've created a dedicated space, ideally a separate room, complete with litter box, toys, and food and water dishes for the new cat. When you bring your new cat home, keep him in that room, with the door closed, for at least two weeks. This gives the "old" cat a chance to get used to the new guy's smell.

Introduce them during a low-stress time, ideally an evening meal. Should a fight start, distract them with a loud noise, or cover one of the cats with a blanket. Relocate your new cat to a different isolation area. Then repeat the exercise until the cats begin to tolerate each other. If it continues to be heavy weather, contact an animal behaviorist. Ideally, your cats will work it out. However, bear in mind that a certain number of multi-cat combinations won't work, and be prepared to remove a cat who isn't working out—and find him a good home.

HOW DOES THIS AFFECT MY CAT'S DIET?

Even if your cats get along like a house afire, a social hierarchy governs all their interactions. Somebody is always top cat, and somebody isn't. Free access to food in a multi-cat household is an invitation to obesity. If you are trying to slim one cat down, make sure that each of your cats has his or her own separate feeding bowl area, and monitor, monitor, monitor.

When thinking about food bowls, don't forget to anticipate the age and mobility of your cats. Is your fat cat an older cat, not so enamored of jumping? Make sure you place the younger, skinnier cats' food up on a counter or a table where your fat cat is less likely to leap. So what if your fat cat has learned to leap on the kitchen counter and eat whatever he sees? Experts recommend immediate intervention. Clap your hands, shout "No, bad cat!" and remove your cat from the counter. The next time you spot your cat on the counter, it may be time to whip out the spray bottle. Get a regular size squirt bottle or plant sprayer and fill it with water and spray it at your feeding feline. She won't like it, but it won't hurt her, either.

HOW MANY CATS AM I ACTUALLY FEEDING?

It sounds like a silly question, but it really isn't. Some cats can be quite aggressive about swiping the food of their less forceful brothers and sisters. Keeping track of exactly what each of your cats is eating is not only a great step toward your fat cat's weight loss—it's also helpful in getting a clear picture of who's eating what.

Measuring your fat cat's food (and water) intake allows you to take control over his food, and gives you an objective benchmark to keep track of his weight. And when we say "food," we mean everything—treats included. Much like the cliché, "broken pretzels don't have calories," many cat owners seem to share a belief that treats somehow have a different caloric count than regular cat food—which is nothing. Treats should make up only 10-15% of your cat's daily nutrition. Make sure to keep track of them, too.

Train your humans, too. One of the largest causes of overweight cats is well-meaning humans who bond with their felines over food. Sometimes lots of food. If children in your family have become conditioned to giving the cat lots of treats, don't cut them off cold turkey. Encourage them to break the treats into smaller pieces. If possible, get them interested in training the cat while using the treat. But if, after some time family members simply "don't get it," it may become necessary to sequester the food and treats in a separate bin or cabinet. If they can't find it, they can't feed it to the cat.

Unless you're sure you're going to get perfect compliance from your people, you may have to stick to training your cat. If you are going to be away for any length of time, and you really, really, want your cat not to jump up on the counter, it's time to construct a booby trap. Alice Rhea, author of *Good Cats, Bad Habits*, recommends booby-trapping the counter with either a noisemaker (such as a group of soda cans filled with gravel), or if you don't want the noise, make the counter wet and uninviting by blanketing the counter top with very wet towels. Pam Johnson-Bennett recommends placing bumpy rubber mats where you don't want the cat to go. High tech solutions include a vibration sensitive cat alarm available from pet supply stores—but they aren't cheap.

It is possible to diet your cat in a multi-cat family; even research supports it. Dr. Emily Levine, D.V.M., one of the lead researchers on the 2004 Cornell "fat cat" diet study, reports that several of the cats who successfully lost weight were from multi-cat families. This works best when your cat family is composed of a skinny cat who likes to jump up to his special place (say, a counter) for his food, and your fat cat eats his diet food on the floor. Freestyle feeding is not recommended when one cat is on a diet and the rest aren't; it becomes almost impossible to monitor and control what any cat is eating. Keep all your cats on schedule, and keep an eye on what they're eating.

MY CAT, MY EXERCISE COACH

If you have an expectation that a new cat will have the old cat scampering around the house, you might be right. But if your new cat is placid, don't be surprised to see the established cat slow down his routine, too. You have to initiate a group play activity, with the goal that the cats play close to, but not right next to, each other. Use two separate toys to achieve this; cats are likely to spar over a single toy. Often, older cats do "parent" younger cats, and usually one cat will serve as a role model for the other.

Also, each cat should have a separate play area—a cat tower of his own, if possible, or shelf or perch. Regardless of what you choose, observe your cats carefully to see exactly how they've mapped out their territory, and follow their lead.

CATS AND DOGS

As with cat-to-cat introductions, introduce cats to dogs (and vice versa) very slowly. Make sure that prior to your pet's arrival at your

Be prepared for a showdown, like this one between Stinky and Loki, when you introduce a new pet into the house.

house, he has his own designated separate space with a door that closes. Bring your new cat or dog home in a carrier, and leave him, still in the carrier, in his room. Bring your old cat or dog in on a leash. Allow him to sniff and explore, but if either animal begins to get stressed out, command your old pet to retreat, and take him out of the room. Close the door. Only then remove the new pet from his carrier in his safe place.

Over the next couple of weeks, allow both dog and cat to get used to each other's scent. After two weeks, put a baby gate across the entry of the safe room. Always let the cat choose how much face time he wants with the dog. If you have any questions about your dog's behavior, keep a leash on him at all times, and remind your dog of all of his basic commands, most especially, "Stay," and "Leave it." Reward him for any and all good behavior with the cat.

Never, ever put a kitten in a room with a grown dog with no supervision. Some kittens like to play a game called "ambush," which plays out exactly the way it sounds, and while the kitten knows he's playing, the dog may not. The dog might pick the little kitten up and shake it, causing nerve damage, or worse.

Here are some basic ground rules for cat-dog peace:
- Never let your dog chase your cat.
- Never let your dog near the litter box. (Some dogs like to snack on the protein-rich leavings.)
- If your dog is a food thief, relocate your cat's food dishes to places the dog can't reach.
- If your cat is a food thief, corral your cat or cats while you feed your dog.

- Expect to have to manage conflict, but be patient.

Even if your cat and dog get along perfectly, adding a dog to your one-cat household may be a hidden culprit in your cat's extra pounds. Why?

Because many dogs are attention hogs, and activity junkies. Dogs beg for walks, for balls, for games of fetch. Unless you have a big yard, and even if you do, you probably walk your dog every day. While your cat…just sits there, quite possibly forgotten in all the playful commotion.

Be aware that there may be a period of adjustment while you get used to your dog's walk schedule, and that it may have an adverse effect on the time you used to spend playing with your cat. Keep an activity log to make sure that you don't stint on your fat cat's exercise.

OTHER PET COMBINATIONS

Most other pet combinations will affect your dieting feline only a little, or perhaps not at all—as long as you attend to the basic rule of cat common sense: Cats are predators. So never, ever introduce a cat to a pet that's the cat's natural prey. This includes snakes, birds, mice, gerbils, and fish.

Putting any cat, especially a dieting cat, in a room with a potential food source is just a bad idea, period. At worst, the cat may attack. At best, you have two very stressed-out animals in the same room. Make sure before you take on a second pet in these categories that you have mapped out safe, separate areas for your new pet, and ascertain that the pet's cage is very secure. It's not impossible to have a Noah's Ark household, but it's vital that you take serious precautions.

SUMMARY

- When introducing a new pet to your cat household, make sure to prepare your home beforehand.
- Expect the adjustment period to last at least two weeks. Let the new cat decide how much he wants to interact.
- Reward immediately for all positive behavior.
- When adding a cat to one-cat home, make sure each cat gets his own "turf," including food bowls, cat furniture, and toys.
- When adding a dog to a one-cat home, keep the dog on a leash until it's clear both animals are getting along. Never leave a kitten alone with an adult dog.

Maintain Your Cat's Healthy Weight

The day is here. It's finally come. Thanks to your hard work and patience, your fat cat has been transformed into a sleek, strong, slim feline. Congratulations!

Just as with human weight loss, however, the key to success is life-long maintenance. Should you find your cat gaining weight again, don't despair. Just go back to the steps outlined in this book:

1. Give your cat a thorough once over, and compare his current body to a picture of him at his optimum weight.

2. Weigh your cat, preferably down to the ounce. Remember that some cats actually "hide" weight. Weigh your cat no more than once a week.

3. Meet with your vet to establish your cat's basic health, as well as a realistic weight loss goal. Remember, slower (2% a week and under!) is better.

4. Establish and maintain a regular feeding schedule—and stick to it. If necessary, select an appropriate diet food. Measure and log in every meal.

5. Let your whole family know that your cat is officially on a diet, and enlist them in the fight to keep your cat slim and healthy.

6. Increase your cat's exercise through structured play, new toys, even training. (Check out Karen Pryor's clicker training books for further information.)

7. Monitor your older cat's progress carefully—too much weight loss too fast is just as dangerous to your cat as being overweight.

8. If your cat's weight gain has been caused by illness or injury, reach out to the Web. The Internet is bursting with all kinds of pet owner communities.

9. Take special care with feeding and exercise when you have multiple pets or if your cat likes to go outdoors.

10. Be patient; nobody gains weight overnight, and nobody loses it that way, either. Not even your brilliant cat.

Just Ten Fat Minutes

For cat owners who are really in a hurry, here are ten tips that take less than ten minutes each to help your cat get trim.

1. Buy a new toy from the Internet.
2. Read the label on your cat food.
3. Spend five minutes playing with your cat and his favorite toy.
4. Buy measuring spoons and cups.
5. Surf the Internet for cat shelves.
6. Start a FAT CAT (food, activity, track/training) log.
7. Join a cat e-mail list devoted to your special kind of cat.
8. Dance down the hall with a low-fat kitty treat until your cat follows.
9. "Retire" one of your cat's toys for a month.
10. Investigate clicker training.

Resources

ADDITIONAL INFORMATION

www.MyFatCatBook.com

For more diet and exercise tips, visit the official *My Fat Cat* Web site. You can also contact the author at Martha@myfatcatbook.com.

VETERINARY RESOURCES

American Animal Hospital Association
www.healthypet.com

The Web site of this international association of over 33,000 veterinary health care providers includes a searchable database of member hospitals, pet care articles, and FAQs about dogs, cats, and other small pets.

American Association of Feline Practitioners
www.aafponline.org

This site offers a directory of member vets who specialize in feline

American Veterinary Medical Association
www.avma.org/careforanimals/default.asp
This 72,000-member organization features downloadable brochures on common cat health issues, as well as information and tips aimed at kids.

The Internet Animal Hospital
www.thepetcenter.com
This dog and cat healthcare site is written and maintained by practicing veterinarians. You can view x-rays of actual cases, see real surgery photos, learn about pet foods and nutrition, and more.

Cornell Feline Health Center
www.vet.cornell.edu/fhc
A fantastic resource for up-to-the-minute academic research, as well as the editorial voice of the readable and informative Cat Watch, a monthly online and paper publication.

American Academy of Veterinary Acupuncture
www.aava.org
Provides a searchable directory of practitioners, as well as links to many members' Web sites.

CAT KNOWLEDGE AND BEHAVIOR
www.messybeast.com
A gigantic, independent, information-rich site run by British cat lover Sarah Hartwell, which she describes as a "not-for-profit archive of information on cat care, welfare, behaviour, breeding, rescue, and feline general interest," not to mention cat history.

www.pamjohnsonbennett.com
The Web site of cat behaviorist Pam Johnson-Bennett, author of such helpful books as *Cat vs. Cat* and *Think Like A Cat.*

www.catagility.com
The home of International Cat Agility Tournaments, this Web site provides training resources, schedules of upcoming events, and many pictures of agile cats having fun.

www.friskies.com
Provides a 4-item guide to creating your own no-budget home agility course—and an even more important 4-step guide to getting your cat interested in your agility course.

www.clickertraining.com/home
The online home of Karen Pryor, one of the leading voices of clicker training. Offers many clicker training products, including fun activity cards…for cats!

ENVIRONMENTAL ENRICHMENT FOR CATS

animalhousestyle.com
The Web site of Julia Szabo, pet and style writer, who shares her home—stylishly, with a group of rescued cats and dogs.

www.pix.tv
The online home of artists Bob Walker, Frances Mooney, and their many, many cats (and one dog). Walker and Mooney have designed their color-rich home, dubbed "The Cats' House," to their cats' activities, with a variety of imaginative shelves, perches, alleys, and hallways—all for cats. A great place for inspiration while thinking about a more cat-friendly house, and living proof that cats and art are good for each other.

SPECIAL NEEDS CATS

www.felinediabetes.com

Not just for cats with diabetes and their owners—though that would be enough—this Web site provides helpful nutritional comparison charts for dry and canned food, and cat snacks.

www.petswithdisabilities.org

Overseen by Joyce Dickerson, who shares her life with several handicapped pets, including a cat who was "adopted" by one of her dogs. Valuable FAQ about dealing with pets in wheelchairs.

www.handicappedpets.com

Created by a pet lover in memory of his late disabled dog, includes access to supplies, wheelchairs, leash/slings, books; features a lively online community.

Recommended Reading

Carlson, Delbert G. and James M. Giffin with Liisa Carlson. *Cat Owner Home Veterinary Handbook.* Howell House, 1995.

Christensen, Wendy. *The Humane Society of the United States Complete Guide to Cat Care.* St. Martin's Press, 2002.

Fogle, Bruce. *The New Encyclopedia of the Cat.* Dorling Kindersley, 2001.

Johnson-Bennett, Pam. *Cat vs. Cat.* Penguin, 2004.

Pitcairn, Dr. Richard and Susan Hubble Pitcairn. *Dr. Pitcairn's Complete Guide to Natural Health for Dogs & Cats.* Rodale, 1995.

Rainbolt, Dusty. *Kittens for Dummies.* Wiley, 2003.

Siino, Betsy Sikora, ed. *The Essential Kitten.* Howell House, 1999.

Spadafori, Gina and Paul D. Pion. *Cats for Dummies, 2nd Edition.* Wiley, 2000.

Sussman, Les. *The American Animal Hospital Association Encyclopedia of Cat Health and Care.* Quill, 1995.

Szabo, Julia. *Animal House Style.* Bulfinch, 2005.

Photo Credits